"If you are in the early years of motherhood, book is for you. Author Leah Spina takes readers on a humorous tour through the normal stages and learning experiences of parenting, including pregnancy, birth, sleepless nights, potty training, and more. The book feels like a conversation with a friend who shares her best and funniest motherhood tales—at times I found myself laughing out loud. And woven through it all, she invites you to reflect and examine how you can 'stop and smell' your children more. There were so many times while reading this book that I thought, 'Exactly!' It was refreshing to hear stories from someone in the exact stage of motherhood I am in. She doesn't sugar coat anything—often revealing her biggest challenges. It felt good to know that I'm not the only one who has struggled with these things."

Sarah Monson, powerofmoms.com

"Most young women and new mamas too often encounter the horror stories of parenting, but, in this oftentimes hilarious and always inspiring book, Leah has turned the terrible into terrific by sharing her stories of parenting with true delight. So if you want to laugh and enjoy, too, stop and buy NOW!"

Shonda Parker, Author of _Mommy Diagnostics: The Art of Taking Care of Your Family_, Speaker, Mother of seven, and grandmother of two
www.naturallyhealthy.org

"After reading Leah's book, I started to slow down and treasure the fleeting, exhausting, happy, chaotic moments of raising my little boys. I saw mundane tasks like changing diapers as opportunities to bond with my boys. Her real life stories are funny but have memorable applications. If you are being swallowed up in the little years like I am, this book will help you slow down, laugh and get a new perspective on ENJOYING your babies! Great gift for new moms!"

Faith Burke, Mother of two boys, age two-and-under

"Leah had me laughing 'til I cried from her relatable experiences of life with little ones. The down to earth stories she shares in her book are therapeutic for every young mother's soul. Leah reminded to appreciate and savor the little moments, which are easy to overlook in the fog of survival. Every young mom will be encouraged by her honest and humorous antidotes. As a mother of two small boys, I highly recommend this book as a must read to all mom's who need a fresh new perspective and a reason to laugh."

Grace Tharp, Mother of two-year-old twins

"I have spent the afternoon mostly laughing, but occasionally shedding tears, as I read Leah's new book, Stop and Smell Your Children. *I loved the real life, down home, spill every-thing approach she used as she recounted lessons she learned both in child rearing and marriage. I read several books a week—this one stands out as a true winner."*

Debi Pearl, Author, Speaker,
Founder No Greater Joy Ministries

"At every page turn of Leah's book, I laughed and then cried, I kept thinking how excited I am for my mom friends to get their own copies. As a mom who knows the blessings I have from the perspective of losing a child, I remember the early days of motherhood—not having my current perspective back then—and wishing away the days of constant meeting the needs of young children need. Yes, the years with little people are so short, and if moms miss that from living out the long days without perspective, they'll miss the greatest gifts in life. This is a must read, and I feel honored to have watched Leah walk out her writings."

Dr. Cindy Haggerton, Speaker, Business Owner,
Mother to four children, age six-and-under

"Do I laugh or do I cry? Laugh, because Leah writes about 'funny stuff.' Cry, because I can relate to her adventures and she touches my heart. By 'stopping,' as Leah advises, moms in the midst of their baby and toddler season can learn a great deal from her valuable insights and will be better able to not only endure these years, but enjoy them as well!"

Shari (and Ted) Pittenger
Founders of Samaritan Ministries International

"The days are long but the years are short. Leah's book is a fun, uplifting and heartwarming reminder of this truth. Upon tiresome days when I've been run down (or run over) by parenting tasks, Stop and Smell Your Children inspires me to change my outlook and find joy in the mundane. It's a funny read too; I even woke up my husband a few times, giggling over Leah's misadventures with Samson and Esther. Every mother with small children needs to buy this book and keep it handy to read for bouts of encouragement throughout the week."

Jennifer Pilgrim, blogger of the ModernPilgrimBlog.com
and Mother to one-year-old, Annabelle

"A treasure of insight and inspiration, Stop and Smell Your Children is a must read. Through laughter and tears, you will see smashed peas and scattered toys as priceless memories, and embrace parenting challenges with new freedom and confidence. I am going to recommend it to every parent of young children I know."

Marci Fish, Mother of four, Speaker, Pastor, Teacher

"I read this entire book in two days. An excellent read for anyone, especially moms of young children! I found myself laughing, crying, and then stopping to revel in the beauty of motherhood. How refreshing to not feel alone in my struggles, and to be encouraged with a fresh perspective and practical ideas! Broken into short chapters that are doable for a busy mom to finish, you will gain nuggets of wisdom as you enjoy Leah's captivatingly, hilarious writing style. Whether you have five minutes or an hour to devote to reading in your day, this book is the perfect choice!"

**Jessica Driggers, Military Mom to three children,
age four-and-under**

"This book is all about laughing at the crazy spills in parenting and turning that moment into a photo op. I love a good photo op! Fantastic! Seeing Leah change those chaotic parenting moments by changing her parenting perspective is encouraging to all the other mothers going through the same crazy. She is so fun and always gives a good laugh! Great read for every new mother ... awesome!

**Shoshanna Easling, Mother of two, age nine and four,
Speaker, Video Personality, and Author of *Making Babies Book:
Fertility, Pregnancy and Birth the Natural Way* and
*Making Babies DVD series***

"*Leah's writing is relatable and encouraging to young parents struggling through the baby and toddler years. Her gift for seeing everyday life with humor and wisdom will leave you laughing and challenge you to maximize these short years with your tots. Definitely worth reading and sharing with all the moms you know!*"

**Rachel Vecera, Mother of a two-year-old boy,
with another baby on the way!**

"*Leah has such a super perspective of children, and not the typical 'can't wait 'til they are grown and gone' mentality. Her creative ways of loving and cherishing these little blessings will encourage you! Her joy and energy is contagious!*"

Hilary Spivey, Mother of five, ages two to fourteen

"*I've enjoyed Leah's style of writing ever since I've been following her stories about her children on Facebook. So when I found out about her book I was extremely excited! This book is entertaining and is exactly what I needed as a new mom to remind myself that these years are so precious, and they fly by very quickly! I have a new perspective and I'm glad that being a mom is not about the perfectly clean home and perfectly groomed kids. I can finally take the pressure off myself … thank you Leah! Your book is fresh air!*"

Michelle Carey, Mother of a one-year-old daughter

"Stop and Smell Your Children *is a delightful look into the genuine heart of author, Leah Spina. I have personally witnessed her growth as a person and as a mother, and seeing her use her experiences to bless and encourage others is a true delight. As a mom of six, I need as many reminders as possible to take moments to find joy and fun, rather than becoming lost in the ongoing tasks that go along with this crazy, busy season. Take a few minutes for yourselves, dear mamas, and laugh and cry your way through this gem of a book!*"

**Courtney Critz, Mother of six children, age 11 and under,
Homeschooling Mom, Speaker, Small Business Owner**

"I don't remember the last time I read half a book at one time at night without falling asleep! (And that's rare for a tired mom of little ones, so that in itself is a compliment to this book!) This is a refreshingly honest and witty account of real life as it unfolded. Full of humor and truth, this book is a testimony of how life can bring true sorrow, but with fresh perspective and new eyes, God can turn that same tragedy into immeasurable joy and gratitude for the future. I laughed and teared up and completely related to Leah's parenting stories. It's nice to know I'm not the only one and that life is how you choose to see it. We blink and it's over. I cannot wait to play with my kids and hold them tighter and longer and find the joy in even the smallest of tasks."

Jill Kirk, Mother to three, age five-and-under

"Stop and Smell Your Children *is a delightful, hilarious, and refreshing book! The captivating stories and profound insights are a breath of fresh air! As a mom of three little ones, I love how the author perfectly captured this crazy wonderful season of motherhood. This book was a wonderful reminder to slow down and intentionally see the good all around me, while embracing the precious little keepsake moments. I now have a deeper love for my children and renewed perspective. I'm cherishing little moments instead of just surviving and getting through the day. This fun and captivating book is a must read!"*

Esther Vermillion, Conference Speaker, Business Owner, and Mother to three, age seven and under

"This is a MUST READ for new parents to help them gain perspective during the young children season—and provides lots of laughs along the way about common parenting experiences! This is also a great read for parents with grown children or grandchildren to reminisce their own fond parenting memories. I laughed out loud many times, and also enjoyed the great parenting hints along the way. Leah's real-life parenting stories are hilarious, honest, and each chapter ending provides a constructive takeaway for parents to apply to their specific season of parenting—whether they are parents-to-be or have multiple young children. It's a fast, easy read, and perfect for the busy, overwhelmed mom to enjoy during naptime or after the kids go to bed. Don't think twice about buying this book. Get it today so you can truly enjoy your children!"

Esther Spina, author *The Ambitious Woman*, Mother to four

"*When Leah blew into Asheville years ago for the World Journalism Institute it was like a Texas tornado had hit town. She was talented, beautiful, vivacious and a force to be reckoned with, even then. Now married to David Spina with little rug rats, she looks like a movie star and writes like Erma Bombeck. Hang on to your ten gallon hats 'cause this Texas filly is about to entertain and inspire you.*"

Robert Case, Founding Director, World Journalism Institute

"*I love Leah's real world advice, and writing style. It's nice to have the perspective of an everyday mom who has taken the time to look at her own life and share what worked and what didn't—so the rest of us can avoid some of the pitfalls, and enjoy more of the good stuff!*"

Jennie-Laurie Hope, Mother to two age six and under, Health and Fitness Coach for Women, and Founder of Hopeful Fitness

"*They say laughter is good medicine and I agree! Leah's perspective will have you laughing about the in and outs of early motherhood. This is a great read for new and seasoned moms. Finding humor in the daily grind of taking care of young children is refreshing.* Stop and Smell Your Children *has me smiling and that's good for my whole family!*"

Monica Brown, Mother of eight children, Entrepreneur ("Mompreneur"), Business Owner, Speaker, Parenting Class Instructor

"Stop and Smell your Children *is an overlooked, vital parenting principle that Leah brings to life from her own mothering experiences. Her humorous and honest parenting stories help busy moms change their parenting perspective to truly enjoy their young children. The overwhelming 'Diaper blizzard' years describe a perspective that older moms wish they could re-do ... similar to the husband who never looks back and wishes he spent more time at his work. We all wish we had intentionally enjoyed our children more!*"

Lynette Driggers, Mother of five, Grandmother of nine age five-and-under, Mom Mentor, Transitional Care Parent for more than 100 babies and young children

Stop and Smell YOUR CHILDREN

laugh and enjoy the little years

Stop and Smell YOUR CHILDREN

laugh and enjoy the little years

LEAH SPINA

NEXT CENTURY
PUBLISHING

Stop and Smell Your Children

Laugh and Enjoy the Little Years

Copyright ©2015 by Leah Spina
All rights reserved.

Published by Next Century Publishing
www.NextCenturyPublishing.com
Las Vegas, NV

ISBN: 978-1-62903-834-6

Library of Congress Control Number: 2015931555

Photography credit: Steve Colwill of Poetic Exposure.

Printed in the United States of America

DEDICATION

First, I dedicate this book to my incredible husband, David Spina. Late one Tuesday night in our destroyed playroom, Dave and I discussed whether or not we should go forward with this book. We were each sprawled out on a chair, utterly exhausted after a long day. I grilled him with my ex-journalist machine-gun cynical questioning.

Finally, Dave, who is *way* better at making big decisions than I am, rested his forehead on his hand and sighed. "Okay, Leah. What's the worst that can happen?"

I smiled sheepishly. "Thousands of unsold books in our garage?"

Dave grinned as big as Texas. "Well, at least you would have lots of gifts for your friends over the next few years."

I burst out of my chair laughing, jumped into his lap and planted a big kiss on his forehead. I may write a lot about my children, but it is my husband who rocks my world. Love you to the moon and back, my love.

Second, I dedicate this book to my darling children, tow-headed preschooler Samson and doll baby Esther. I hope these stories convey how much I enjoy you each day. I cannot wait for the precious years ahead, but I bask in the everyday joy you both give me. Samson, I am so proud of your strong and hilarious personality that makes me laugh each day. I love reading picture books with you in our special spot by the window. Esther, just last week I asked your daddy if perhaps you were an angel instead of a little girl who God gave us—you are that sweet. You're a ball of smiley sunshine who lights up our home and our lives. I love you both with all my heart. Nothing you can do will ever make me stop loving you.

Third, I dedicate this book to my two sets of parents. To my mom and dad, Richard and Lynette Driggers, who enjoyed their five children more than any parents I know, thank you for breathing character, faith and love into us year after year. Mom, you are the quintessence of the ideal mother with angelic love for all. When I am sick, I still want my mama to take care of me; you always stroked my forehead with compassion and never forgot to pop a colorful straw in my drink to make hydration cheery. Dad, remember the Saturday when that snooty state-champion girl trounced me in a tennis tournament 6-0, 6-0, and I crawled off the court dejected? You ran over to me, grabbed my slumped shoulders and wagged your finger in my teenage face, saying, "The only difference between you and that girl is a couple of thousand more tennis balls. That's it. She's just played a little bit more than you." Because of that and many other pivotal parenting moments, I graduated high school believing I could do anything in life. I love and admire you both. You are the best parents in the whole world!

To my parents-in-love, Frank and Esther Spina, who told me to write a book and made me do it. Dad, thanks for always listening patiently to my big ideas. When I talk to you, I always feel like I'm the only person in the room. Thank you for wrestling Samson on the living room rug and for snuggling Esther on your lap to read baby board books. Mom, I will never forget that Friday night when gave me a fiery book pep talk in your upstairs home office. When I left, you called down to me, "Send in that manuscript tonight or I'm not talking to you tomorrow." Thank you both for believing in me and encouraging me to achieve my dreams, and for allowing my kids to wreak havoc in your gorgeous home any time of day or night. I'm really sorry about the one hundred multi-colored blocks they leave out every time we come over.

I also dedicate this book to my spunky redheaded aunt, Carolyn Driggers Mallone, who is now with the Lord. When I was a teenager and young adult, you took me out for lunch at a starched-tablecloth restaurant every November to celebrate my birthday. As the oldest of five children, that special outing in my honor made me feel like the queen of England. Without fail, sometime during our meal, you would take off your big black celebrity glasses, look me straight in the eye across the table and confidently state, "You are an incredible writer and you need to write. You are going to write a book someday." Here it is, Aunt Carolyn! I only wish you could be here to read it.

Finally, thank you, God, for showing me that each precious day is a gift from you. Help me to be wise in using my time. Help me to also be others-focused, even when my family is so endearing. Help me to see the lost and hurting as you see them. Help me to show your love to one and all. Thank you for this unmitigated happiness in young children. You are good and your works are good. Blessed be your name.

Table Of Contents

Stop and Smell
YOUR CHILDREN
laugh and enjoy the little years

FOREWORD

Welcome to the club known as parenthood.

Maybe you're pregnant and vomiting your eyeballs out, or perhaps you're reading this as a red-eyed zombie from too many sleepless nights with a newborn. Or maybe it's only 7 p.m. and you just fell into bed fully clothed because you're too exhausted to put on pajamas after a long day of caring for multiple young children.

This book is for you, new parent. If anyone needs to laugh instead of cry, you do. If anyone needs a friend in the trenches cheering them on, it's the what-have-I-gotten-myself-into mom. If anyone needs help to see the beauty in the diaper chaos, it's the I-haven't-got-a-clue dad.

I wrote this book for you because I don't want you to just survive the little years; I want you to thrive and love them. I have learned—through loss and life—just how important it is to slow down and enjoy my young children, and that has changed my life.

The parenthood club is one of the greatest and most rewarding clubs you will ever join. So welcome, fellow new parent, to the experience of your lifetime.

INTRODUCTION

I have two small children as I type these words. When we brought our second child home from the hospital, I started to lose it. My home constantly looked like a bankrupt daycare, I had to change my dirty, child-dominated clothes four times a day and I never left the house except to get the mail—and that was on a good day.

Parenting young children can be like a never-ending circus: the messes, the needs, the interruptions, the toy chaos, the emotional toddler, the crying baby, the diaper parade. I hated the person I was becoming. I snapped at the people I loved the most, my husband and children. At night I sobbed to Dave that I was barely surviving each day and prayed I could make it through the next one. I wasn't enjoying my children or my life. Something had to change.

That something was my parenting perspective. I was desperate and determined to smile and laugh in the midst of the bedlam. I didn't want to just survive these years; I wanted to enjoy them. While I couldn't change my circumstances, I could change my perspective. Each day I started to search for extraordinary, ordinary parenting moments. I started to see humor instead of defeat in the diaper war. Now I try to treasure each day with my little ones as a gift to savor instead of a duty to endure.

I wish I could come clean your house for you, take over baby night duty so you could sleep eight glorious hours, cook you a hot meal *and* clean up your kitchen afterward, watch your kiddos so you could enjoy a long uninterrupted shower and take care of your laundry with a Mary Poppins snap. (Unfortunately, I can't because I'm too tired to do it for my own family. Ha!) But

I can offer you my stories—the nitty-gritty details of my new parent struggles, the lessons I've learned and the perspective I've gained that has forever changed me as a parent.

Perhaps tonight you'll read this book after you tuck away your little angels and then tomorrow *you* will discover your own extraordinary ordinary parenting moment. Maybe after your toddler spills milk in the car, you will laugh instead of cry. Perhaps you will stop to kiss your baby while changing a diaper. Your children will only be small for a short time. Laugh and enjoy the little years!

I wrote this book during my children's naptime—the golden hours when they were asleep simultaneously—and after their bedtime. I tucked them in, kissed their button lips and stumbled into the kitchen to down a six-ounce Starbucks Doubleshot Espresso in 2.5 seconds. I then trudged upstairs to the demolished playroom and collapsed into my old black office chair and booted up my laptop on a desk decorated with Sharpie-marker drawings. I could have waited five years to write this book, but then I would've forgotten what it was like in this crazy but magical season of parenting little ones. And I never, *ever* want to forget!

CHAPTER ONE

The Pregnancy Test

"A grand adventure is about to begin."

–Winnie the Pooh

Dave and I were vacationing at the beach on the day we found out we were pregnant. The morning sun filtered in through the white faux-wood window blinds and woke me. Next to me, Dave snoozed on his side like a black bear hibernating, an ivory pillow covering his face and the navy-striped comforter pulled over his broad shoulders. I got up to use the bathroom and then slipped back into bed. Moments later, I realized that my period was late.

I shook Dave and ripped off his face pillow like the intense, bad-timing wife that I am. "Honey! I think I'm pregnant! I'm a day late! I've been charting six months and I've never gone this long!"

Dave yawned without opening his eyes. "What about all the months before that?"

Our vacation would end later that day, so we decided to wait until we got home to take a pregnancy test. That night we strolled into our neighborhood Walmart across stained concrete floors to buy one.

"Do you know where the pregnancy tests are located?" he asked.

I stared at him, taken aback. "No! I've never taken a pregnancy test before. What kind of girl do you think I am?"

After some searching, we discovered them by the feminine products, further embarrassing my ultra-masculine husband. "What kind should we get?" he asked.

Who knew there were so many different tests to choose from? "I literally have no idea," I said.

Dave grabbed a box. "Here's a two-pack. Let's go."

As soon as we jumped in the car, I ripped open the plastic wrapper and read the instructions aloud on the drive home. It seemed simple enough. One line meant not pregnant, two lines meant pregnant. Wait three minutes to get the results. The test was most accurate first thing in the morning. Oh, dear … the sun was setting.

"Well, we *did* buy a two-pack," Dave pointed out. "So we could try one tonight and one again tomorrow morning." Now that was thinking.

When we arrived home, I dashed into our bathroom and yelled to Dave, "Honey, can you time three minutes on your iPhone?"

"Sure!"

"Okay, start timing!"

But as soon as I set the test on the counter to process, a second pink line appeared.

I gasped. "Honey! Come quick!"

Dave bolted in and his eyes grew wide. "Aren't we supposed to wait three minutes?"

"Yeah, okay," I stammered. With two lines already showing, what would change in three minutes? But then again, this was my first pregnancy test.

Dave placed his phone next to the pregnancy test stick on the bathroom counter. We huddled over them like two novice fertility scientists, silently watching the phone timer count down and the pink lines deepen in color.

After the three longest minutes of my life, I screamed for joy inside but tried to remain calm. "Well?"

Dave paused for a moment, then looked at me, his brow furrowed. "Take another one. We need to make sure."

"Um, I don't need to use the restroom anymore."

"Well, you'll just have to drink lots of water!"

I started to head for the kitchen, but then hesitated like a shrewd intellectual. "But won't that dilute the results?" Even so, it was worth a chance. I drank more water than a dehydrated desert camel and took a second test. This one again showed the coveted two magical lines.

We were going to have a real live baby!

We embraced in the kitchen like a couple does at the end of a good romantic movie. I was so excited I could hardly breathe. Then I realized that life would never be just Dave and me anymore. I pulled back to stare him in the eye. "Honey, is it going to be okay?"

Dave beamed. "Of course!"

We decided to tell the whole family our news at a family dinner at the Olive Garden that night. (Classy choice for announcing our little olive, don't you think?) Dave and I drove in stunned silence to the restaurant. It was still so surreal. Suddenly he said, "Leah! Are you sure it was *two* lines that means pregnant or was it *one* line? Did you get it right?"

I gasped in panic, then sputtered, "Oh, Dave! Don't do this to me! I'm pretty sure I got it right!"

I had got it right. The next morning, we emailed a cheesy announcement to our friends—a photo of Dave and me holding a diaper with the words "Tiny diapers arriving soon, we're having a baby in June!" scribbled on it with a black Sharpie marker. We were going to be parents.

Stop and Smell: Children change everything. Once a baby arrives, our lives are no longer our own, but what a beautiful sacrifice. We get to experience the world through the eyes of an innocent, precious tiny human. As the baby grows, we gain a companion by our side as we go about our day—a built-in little buddy. Embrace the change and welcome your wonderful new normal.

Stop and Reflect:

1. How did you feel when you first learned you were going to have a baby?

2. What were you the most excited about?

3. What scared you the most?

4. Try writing down your story. It will be a sweet, fun memory to enjoy for the rest of your life!

CHAPTER TWO

The Morning Sickness Monster

"If men got pregnant, morning sickness would rank as the nation's #1 health problem."

–Anonymous Mother

I enjoyed six weeks of blissful pregnancy until the Morning Sickness Monster attacked. Whoever named it *morning* sickness lied. For me, it was *all-day-and-all-night* sickness. I vomited at least once daily for four months and then sporadically until delivery. In between, I was constantly nauseated. Welcome to motherhood, *dah*ling.

The only thing I could keep down were Coke Slurpees. I knew the location of every 7-Eleven within a fifty-mile radius. Riding in a car made me sick, so when Dave drove, I unashamedly stuck my head out of the window, hoping the fresh air would keep the nausea at bay. I'm sure I looked like one of those dogs—head out the window, eyes half closed and cheeks flapping in the fifty-mile-per-hour wind.

Morning sickness was the best diet on the planet for me. Instead of gaining weight, I lost a whopping twenty pounds in four months from all the vomiting. I tried everything to get relief—drugs, acupuncture, chiropractic care, massage (I felt so light-headed post massage that I had to call Dave to come pick me up), wrist sea bands, raw ginger, and my personal favorite, beans of every variety. Nothing worked.

One morning I pulled into a Starbucks drive-through line, hoping to order something to ease the rampant nausea. Right after two cars pulled behind me, I realized in horror that I was going to vomit right then and there. As the car in front of me moved forward, I shoved my car door open and vomited right there on the pavement in front of everyone. I knew I couldn't just stay in line, barfing instead of ordering, so I wiped the drool off my chin with the back of my hand, put my car in reverse and turned to motion for the stunned drivers behind me to back away.

Finally, the cars backed up and I floored it into the closest parking spot and finished throwing up. As I sat there, shaking from the aftermath, I burst out laughing. Surely everyone in the line thought that it was a hangover puke. Hello, pregnancy!

I also became a super sleuth of smells. In the kitchen I could still detect the aroma of a meal I'd made two days before. I recoiled at the smell of laundry detergent on Dave's clothes. And at restaurants I smashed fourteen lemon slices into my ice water glass, desperately hoping the citrus smell and taste would distract me from smelling every meal that came out of the kitchen.

Grocery store scents triggered sickness the quickest of all. I got really good at shopping while holding my nose, but that didn't always work. One afternoon I tore out of Walmart, sprinting like a preggo track star. But when I reached my car, I had nowhere to hide. I yanked open the car door and, with one hand gripping the top of the door and the other white-knuckling the top of the car, began vomiting. It was an especially loud and long event.

When I finished, I slowly raised my head like a cautious giraffe to discover three paralyzed shoppers staring at me with dropped jaws as they gripped their shopping carts in shock. One yelled from a safe distance, "Do you need help?"

Panting softly, I yelled back, "I'm pregnant," and then crumbled into my car.

At home I threw up so often that even our dog ignored it. When I got discouraged, Dave was quick to encourage me: "Want me to tell you a story I read in my military combat book about how rats were trained, through suffering, to handle adversity better in the long run?" Thanks, love.

Even so, there was a silver lining. I read that vomiting developed abs of steel. So when I vomited, I pretended I was an Olympic vomiting champion training for the abs gold. "Come on, is that the best you have?" I yelled at my white porcelain toilet while kneeling with a death grip on the sides.

Surely when my baby was born, it would all be worth it.

Stop and Smell: Sometimes in parenthood, we face tough seasons: morning sickness, cranky teething babies, potty training marathons, sleepless nights, back-to-back ear infections, and much more. We can't always control or change our circumstances, but we can change our attitude. As parents we can either laugh or cry—and sometimes both at the same time!—and we can either focus on the bad with despair or seek out the good with a smile. Try to find the good in your day as a parent!

Stop and Reflect:

1. What is one funny story you recall from your pregnancy?

2. What was the hardest part of pregnancy for you?

3. What part(s) of pregnancy did you enjoy?

CHAPTER THREE

Maternity Jeans, Old-Lady Shoes And Birthing Videos

"Danger: Due to the influence of pregnancy hormones, I could burst into tears or kill you in the next 5 minutes. You have been warned."

—someecards[1]

Even on the hardest days of battling the Morning Sickness Monster, I made myself think about friends who couldn't have children. Each Mother's Day and Father's Day reminded them of their empty homes. I also thought of friends who were still single but longed for marriage and children. How could I complain when these friends would have given anything to be happily married to a caring husband and have a healthy baby growing inside them each day? They would've traded places with me at a moment's notice.

Plus, there were also some pregnancy perks ... like my new curvy figure. One morning while in our bedroom, Dave, staring at the floor, muttered, "So, um, are those, um, *permanent?*"

---

[1] http://www.someecards.com/usercards/viewcard/MjAxMi03OTU-4OTc2MDc1MTgyMzNj

"No. Actually, I think they get saggy and small after children. Furthermore, they are really sensitive right now, so don't get any ideas."

When my waistline started to expand too, I proudly bought my first pair of pregnancy jeans with that tan piece of stretchy material that pulls up over the belly. I found them comfortable at first, but every time I sat down and then got up, the jeans fell down a little and I had to jerk them back up into place. (You *know* what I'm talking about, ladies.) If I was at home, I could simply pull them back up since no one was watching. But in public I tried to be a bit more discreet. When I got out of the car in a parking lot, I scanned the area like a robber about to raid a store to ensure no one was watching. When the coast was clear, I yanked up my pants like a crazed, wooden Pinocchio puppet hopping around. I would then smooth my blonde hair back from my oily preggo-hormone face and saunter into the store as confidently as I could with my big belly leading the way.

There was an unanticipated belly perk. All my life I'd always wanted to ride one of those motorized scooters at the grocery store. Pregnancy was the golden ticket. One day during my third trimester, I fell into one (because at that point you have no ab control) at our local Walmart. Dave laughed so hard at me, tootling around with my billowing gray pregnancy dress fluttering behind, that he took a photo and sent it to my entire family.

I got my revenge when we played a doubles tennis match when I was eight months along. I just stood at the net since I could barely move, laughing as he covered the entire court and ran like a mad man chasing the ball.

I admire you women who wear heels when you're pregnant. I couldn't. If I didn't wear comfortable shoes, my feet ached and my ankles ballooned. I felt like a ninety-year-old grandma as I pawed through the shoe department looking for comfortable support shoes. I bought brands I never knew existed, like Naturalizer and Aerosoles. When I checked out, I noticed the chirpy, skinny girl next to me buying a pair of red-hot stilettos. My shoes? I looked like I was a manager at McDonald's.

Being in public posed new challenges. One thing I didn't know was that pregnancy invites perfect strangers to touch, talk to and caress your pregnant belly while diving into long-winded personal sagas of their own pregnancies. At a baby shower, I was sitting next to a friend who also endured tough pregnancies when a mother of two grown children rattled off her amazing experiences with pregnancy, labor *and* delivery. After she laughed and delighted in her own awesomeness, an awkward pause followed. Finally, my dry-witted friend broke the silence: "Well. You sound like a birthing champion."

And then there's the oft-repeated advice, "Oh, get your sleep in now before the baby comes!" Seriously, who sleeps through the night in the latter half of pregnancy? It's like trying to get comfortable with seven pillows with an oversized bowling ball attached to your abdomen. It takes five minutes just to turn over. And just when you get comfortable, you have to go to the bathroom. *Again.* Mainly because your bladder is squished to the size of your grandmother's tomato pin cushion.

So you go the bathroom, then climb—not hop—back into bed and ... good grief, what is *that*? The worst Charley horse spasm of your life attacks you, because your blood is not flowing like it used to. Oh, the pain! Sleep? What sleep?

I soon realized that my sleeplessness was also affecting my poor husband. One morning, after a particularly bad night, I turned over and said to Dave, "Don't worry, honey. Only a few more months of this and then I'll be waking you *every three hours* to feed the wee babe."

He got back at me though. When the baby started really moving, I would get annoyed at the nighttime kickboxing matches. But Dave proudly cooed, "This baby is his father's son. A night owl!"

As the pregnancy progressed, like a true type-A first-time mom, I made Dave watch *The Business of Being Born*, a documentary on the birth process in America. I popped a bag of microwave popcorn and we sat on our brown leather couch, neither of us knowing what to expect. It was a bit graphic, showing both hospital and home births, and we watched in stunned silence. Halfway through, a scene showed a naked, hairy husband in an herbal bath with his laboring wife pressed up against him. Dave pointed at the TV screen and shouted, "I am *not* doing that!"

We soon enrolled in a natural childbirth class. My mother birthed most of her five children at home with a midwife, and I hoped to follow suit, but at a birthing center. On the first Tuesday of class, Dave and I filed into our local birthing center with other expectant mothers and fathers. Couples plopped down on the random chairs and maroon couches, and some even sat on the wood floor.

I discreetly studied the crowd. Who were these people, like us, choosing pain over medication? Everyone seemed friendly, happy and excited about natural birth. But "natural" didn't necessarily translate to "courageous." When the graphic birthing video began, the husband next to me buried his face in his hands and never looked up. During a particularly gritty scene, Dave leaned over and whispered, "Don't worry, honey. I've delivered fifteen puppies."

The instructor then asked the ladies to lie down on colorful Pilates mats and had the husbands simulate painful contractions by squeezing and releasing pressure on his wife's leg. I fake coughed to disguise my burst of laughter while everyone else nodded seriously. She instructed the ladies to breathe slowly and relax through the pain while the husbands counted to ten, gradually squeezing harder and harder and then easing off. This was the best class ever. Dave towered over me, laughing like an evil cartoon villain. "Don't worry, honey. Mary gave birth in a stable. You can handle this."

The class was, in all seriousness, constructive and helpful in educating us on what to expect. The instructor intelligently fielded questions from all the parents-to-be and patiently walked us through the various stages of labor and delivery. She even addressed postpartum care. It was comforting to have some idea of what was to come.

When she started our discussion on nursing, she reminded us that we didn't need to remember every jot and tittle. In front of the whole class, Dave raised his hand and asked, "I'm sorry, but did you just say jot and *tit*-le?" Then came the lactation video, demonstrating proper nursing techniques. Smiling women showed us different ways to position the baby while nursing, including the football hold. Dave whispered, "That's the one I will use." The video concluded with a well-endowed bleached-blonde babe chiming, "So remember, just think happy thoughts. Relax and let the milk flow!" At the back of the class, Dave and I could not stop giggling.

(However, I didn't find it funny when I started nursing and had difficulty. My ever-vigilant husband would enter the room and chant in a high-pitched voice over and over, "So remember, just think happy thoughts. Relax and let the milk flow!" If I hadn't been holding our new baby, I would have thrown a shoe at him.)

Stop and Smell: Parenthood requires incredible sacrifice. On bad days, I call it forced selflessness. No matter how much we want a break, we can't take one. We must persevere and confront our worst faults straight in the face (for me, it was lack of patience). Some seasons can feel like they will break us, like habitual sleep deprivation. But when we make a corny joke as we grab our fourth cup of coffee, we win. We are rolling with the punches and changing. Parents are some of my favorite people because we all survive the same challenges and emerge changed for the better. You can do it!

Stop and Reflect:

1. How did you/do you handle people who wanted to touch or talk to your belly?

2. How did/do you and your partner prepare for birth?

3. What food cravings did you/do you encounter while pregnant?

CHAPTER FOUR

Beached Whale – The Last Trimester

"That moment when you are walking around, actually feeling like you look attractive while pregnant, and then realizing there are cookie crumbs on your belly."

– someecards[2]

You know you're in your third trimester when you drop something on the floor and stare at it for several seconds, thinking, *Do I really need that?* Trying to sleep through the night in later pregnancy is like trying to catch a nap in the middle of Times Square with your own personal Riverdance troop inside your belly. And shoes? I lived exclusively in one pair of squishy Crocs flip-flop sandals for the last month of pregnancy during the steaming Texas summertime.

Looking back I wonder if I had lost my mind at times during my last trimester. For instance, I thought playing in a doubles tennis league with Dave while eight months pregnant was a magical idea—until I had to pick up a ball. I felt like a hippo performing a ballet plié.

---

2   http://www.someecards.com/usercards/unsubmitted/MjAxMy-1iNjM0OTYwYTlkYTgyNWI0

I was also pumped about our "babymoon" vacation—the trendy last trip a couple takes before the baby arrives—until I read in bold lettering under almost every excursion activity, from Jeeps to dune buggies to horseback riding: "No pregnant guests allowed." I tried to break the news gently to my high-activity husband. "So, honey, instead of the beach ATVs, would you like to tour Mexican ruins? I think there is a snack buffet." We made an odd touring couple: the fit young husband and his waddling mammoth wife.

But these times were offset by magical moments of feeling my baby move—for me, one of the sweetest gifts of pregnancy. Then the baby would get the hiccups when I was trying to sleep. Not quite so sweet.

As my due date neared, some of my friends raved about the wonders of cloth instead of disposable diapers. I thought I should at least responsibly broach the subject with Dave so we could research all our options. While we rode in the car one Saturday, I turned to him when we were halfway to our destination. He seemed to be in a good mood, so I figured it was an optimal time to ask his opinion on yet another baby decision.

"So honey … some of my friends told me about the benefits of cloth diapers, like how it prevents diaper rash and—"

"No, sir," Dave interrupted, his eyes never leaving the road. "I am not cleaning poop out of diapers."

I laughed. "Well, okay then. That's the way I was leaning, but I just wanted to make sure we were on the same page." One less thing to decide!

(Freebie: There are so many decisions new parents need to make—sleep training or not, co-sleeping or crib, nursing or formula, natural delivery or epidural, how to handle vaccinations, etc.—and all sorts of fierce Facebook mom wars to make you feel terrible no matter what you decide. I recommend researching your options, making a decision, and then concentrating your energy on important things like enjoying your child! Some of my friends loved cloth diapering, but it just wasn't for us. And guess what? We didn't break up over Pampers. Let others be different. I love supportive mom friends!)

You know you're in your third trimester when you wear your dress backward all day long, arrive at your first errand without your purse, and accidently go into the men's bathroom twice because of pregnancy brain fog. And the out-of-control preggo emotions? I cried at every sappy commercial and through three and a half solid hours of Charlton Heston's movie *The Ten Commandments*. Dave walked in halfway through the movie, chomping on a turkey sandwich, and stared at me. I looked up at him with tears streaming down my cheeks and declared, "It is just ... just such a beautiful story!"

I had no control over this foreign body I now lived in. When I laughed, I wet my pants. When I walked, I passed gas. One time my pregnant friend and I were sitting at my Christmas dinner party. About half a dozen of us were left relaxing in our living room. I was dressed up in pearls and a fun red dress, feeling halfway normal despite my huge belly. Suddenly there was a quiet lull in the conversation and you-know-what happened—I emitted a terribly unladylike sound.

Instead of covering for his pregnant wife, Dave shot an incredulous look across the room at me. "Really? Really, Leah?"

My friend and I burst out laughing, causing her pregnant body to emit the same sound.

Last but not least was the perk of going past my due

date. Everyone answered my call on the first ring. I got so tired of countering the inevitable question that I finally changed my voicemail: "Hi, this is Leah Spina and we have *not* had the baby yet. Oh, wait, what's that pressure? I've got to go. Leave a message!" *Beep.*

Stop and Smell: Parenthood can humble you quicker than a dog can lick a dish. Yes, that's my child throwing a tantrum in the middle of the store, flailing on the ground out of control. Why, yes, that's baby spit-up you smell as we all take off for our three-hour flight. There's nothing I can do. I don't have any more clothes for her! What? My son hit four children in the class? He's never done anything like that at home.

Chin up, shoulders back and smile proudly. You birthed a human and sometimes you have no control over the consequences.

Stop and Reflect:

1. How did you feel in the last stages of pregnancy?

2. What were some of your favorite moments? Funny moments?

3. When did you go into labor—early, late, on time, or scheduled?

4. If you're newly pregnant, how do you feel about the changes you are going through?

CHAPTER FIVE

Labor And Delivery Are From Mars

"Giving birth is little more than a set of muscular contractions granting passage of a child... Then the mother is born."

—Erma Bombeck

I labored for a whopping fifty-two hours with my first child, starting at a birthing center with a midwife and ending up in a hospital receiving pain medication. Oh, and did I mention I was *ten* days overdue?

The day my labor started, I knew something was different when I had to stop periodically in the parking lot of Einstein Bros Bagels just to breathe through contractions. At 3 a.m. the next morning, they were too strong to sleep through, even with Tylenol PM.

I endured one particularly strong contraction and moaned, "Dave, it huuurts!"

Dave stroked my shoulder and quipped, "You have Eve to thank for that." That man should write Hallmark cards.

At 5 a.m. we drove through the dark, quiet night to the birthing center where the same midwife my mother had used in the 1980s waited for us. When we arrived, we took walks and tried different positions as the contractions intensified. She taught us that contractions were most effective if I could relax through the pain. One time I started tensing up during a particularly gritty contraction, so Dave reminded me, "Honey, reeelax."

I snapped back through clenched teeth, "*You* relax!"

I'm not sure what other women feel during labor, but I felt like a featured African animal on a *National Geographic* special. The birth process was primitive and raw, totally out of my control, and totally gross at times. Some of my friends reveled in it, calling it beautiful and natural. All I wanted was my panties on and my body back to myself.

I found I labored best alone. Every time some kind person entered the room to check on me, I hissed, "Do not touch me and do not talk to me."

At 8:30 p.m. the midwife checked me. I was still only five centimeters dilated, my water had not broken and the baby was still positioned high. The midwife advised us that if I didn't progress in the next hour, it would be time to head to the hospital. Another hour passed and nada.

Dave and I climbed into our white Suburban and started the trek to plan B, the hospital. I was thrilled to be driving toward The End. After I was admitted, a male doctor whom I had never met walked in the room and shook my hand. "Why, hello, Mrs. Spina. Let's check our progress." *Let's check our progress?* My foot. *I* was about to be checked. And checked by that same hand of yours that I just shook that shook mine so matter-of-factly.

(Why does everyone act so nonchalant about a woman being checked? I wanted to shout, "Being checked is *so gross!* I'm so sorry you have to do this!" But the nurses and doctors just snapped the plastic gloves on, cool as ice. "I'm going to check you now, Mrs. Spina." Next time I think I'll answer back just as coolly, "Well, have at it, sweetie.")

Speaking of hospitals, every ounce of dignity goes right out the door when you pull on that paper-thin pastel blue hospital gown with the gaping holes in the back. Maybe they know we preggos would never attempt to escape, dressed like that and with nothing on underneath, so we *have* to push the baby out. I mean, even fugitives get orange clothes in jail. Well played, hospital.

Finally, the doctor broke my water and then started Pitocin, the medication used to induce labor and strengthen contractions, since my poor uterus was shot. I had witnessed many births on Pitocin in my previous work as a labor and delivery coach, so I knew that drug-induced contractions were contractions on steroids. They looked like a horrific, red repeating roller coaster on the monitor. My resolve to do the deed *au natural* started to go down the drain. I was exhausted from no sleep and little to eat or drink, and the grisly medicated contractions kept hitting me like balls from a fast-speed batting cage pitching machine, with no let up. I became delirious and yelled at the kind midwife who delivered my mother's babies, "You *caused* this pain!" (When she later visited me after the baby was born, I was so mortified to see her again after my atrocious labor conduct that I kept my eyes glued to the ground and barely spoke.)

Suddenly, I remembered the magic word—*epidural*. I hollered at the sweet young nurse that I wanted an epidural *now*. Dave, remembering our pre-labor talk, tried to remind me I was committed to a natural birth. Like a wild caged animal backed into a corner, I turned from him to face the nurse with as much authority as I could while sporting a hospital gown, with wild hair and no underwear. I raised my voice, purposely and slowly stating my full name for added authority: "I, Leah Grace Spina, the patient, want an epidural NOW!"

That did the trick. The nurse ordered an epidural.

(It's not at all nerve-wracking when the anesthesiologist administers the epidural, is it? "Mrs. Spina, please arch your back like a cat and remain perfectly still while we stick a huge needle right next to your spine, hopefully before another contraction hits and jars the needle." Pshaw.)

After some time, a nurse checked me again. I was dilated to eight centimeters. Incredibly, I remained at eight for the next eleven hours. I looked down at my belly the next morning in shock. I couldn't believe I was still pregnant. Would this ever end? The medical staff starting talking about a C-section. *Are you kidding me?* I thought. *I go through all of this, then have surgery?*

Finally, I heard the most beautiful words from the new nurse: "You're at 9.5." I choked back sobs as grateful tears streamed down my face.

Then the baby's heart rate dropped. Those slowed heartbeats were the most awful sounds I had ever heard. The nurse slammed a red button on the wall and yelled for another nurse. They jammed an oxygen mask on my face. Talk about breathing with a purpose! I gulped long, slow breaths and prayed, *Oh, Lord, please help the baby!* The heart rate stabilized, but I realized then that it wasn't over until the baby was out.

The doctor warned us that some women still require a C-section even after this much progress because, after a lengthy labor, they have no energy left to push. *C'mon, Doc,* I thought, breathing like Darth Vader in my plastic oxygen mask. *Don't talk like that. I'm a tough Texas girl. Let's get this baby out!*

Finally, it was time to push. GAME ON. I ordered everyone around like a birthing diva, telling them how to hold my leg, how to give me oxygen, etc. I wasn't about to waste one extra movement in anticipation of the chance to finally push. Every ounce of my athleticism and competitiveness, born of years playing sports, kicked into gear. I could finally *do* something to get the baby out versus trying to "relax" through the pain. Dave held one leg, the nurse held the other, and I started pushing for three sets of ten seconds.

They set up a mirror, and we all watched as a little blonde-haired head appeared. I pushed the head out with all my might, and the doctor smiled at Dave. "Does it look like a girl or boy head?"

I screamed at him, "Just get the baby ouuuuut!" With another mighty push, the shoulders appeared and, *plop*, there was our precious wet, slimy eight-pound-thirteen-ounce baby.

The doctor turned to Dave. "Well, Daddy, what is it?"

Dave beamed at me like he'd just won the lottery. "It's a boy!"

It was then I collapsed emotionally and physically. It was over. I had borne my husband a son. A manchild. The nurse wrapped the baby and brought him to my side, all swaddled like an angel baby, then asked if I wanted to hold him for the first time.

"No," I snapped back like an angry hyena. "Just give me food and water like I've been asking you to for the past ten hours."

The surprised nurse stared at me, holding my beautiful baby in her arms, then looked at Dave. "Uh ... Does *Daddy* want to hold the baby?"

Dave ripped his shirt off to give the baby skin-to-skin contact as instructed. (I wanted to strangle the nurse-nazies who allowed me only sporadic spoonfuls of ice for sustenance. Who is with me on this? I'm supposed to push another human out of my body on *ice chips*?)

I was exhausted. I had pushed out a gigantic baby in fifteen minutes flat after enduring fifty-two hours of labor. All I wanted to do was be still. But the nurse wanted me to go the bathroom. How dare she ask me to go to the bathroom after all that. *You go to the bathroom*, I wickedly thought.

Dave texted the news of Samson's birth to our praying family while I lay lifeless, like a soldier who had survived a major battle. "Hey, Dave," I said, smiling without opening my eyes. "Did you know that in some countries when a woman births a manchild, they build a shrine in her honor and she never works again?"

(P.S. No one told me about the red button. I discovered it in my hospital post-delivery room. It's the magical Sleep Button. You tap it in the middle of the night when your baby is crying and an angel nurse appears and whisks the wailing newborn out of the room. *Bang*—the delicious sound of your hospital room door closing, followed by darkness and silence. I think I would pay ten thousand dollars to bring that red button home).

The next day, after glorious sleep and food, the nurse brought Baby Samson in to me. For the first time, I slowly reveled in this precious gift from above. I stroked his blonde hair, kissed his little eyes, studied his squishy cheeks, fingered the tiny toes, and celebrated my incredible baby.

Riding home, Dave and I kept darting looks back to that out-of-place new car seat with a tiny baby in it. He looked small and so surreal. We were proud parents now.

Stop and Smell: All labor and delivery experiences are not like mine, of course. Many of my friends have had amazing birth experiences. I've even heard of some labors that lasted only two hours! But that's the great thing about the parenthood adventure. Everyone's experiences are different throughout their unique, little-people journey. Have fun comparing—and laughing—about the differences with other parents. Enjoy getting to know your fellow parenting club members!

Stop and Reflect:

1. What was the hardest part of your labor and delivery?

2. Were there any funny moments?

3. What was your favorite part of your birth story?

4. How did your spouse react during the various stages?

5. If you have time, write out your story. Your child may want to hear it someday.

6. If you are pregnant, what are some of the things you are looking forward to when you deliver?

CHAPTER SIX

Life as a Milkmaid

"I wanted to be ready.
I had thought I was ready.
I really believed I was ready.
That is, until the milk came."

–Kathryn Michaels, *Crazy for Milk*

(Freebie: Mothers may find this chapter a *tad* more intriguing than fathers.)

No one prepared me for the wonders of nursing. I thought it would be like those beautiful colorful Renaissance oil paintings that depict a fat happy mother nursing her fat happy child. Good thing Leonardo da Vinci didn't get me for a mom. The gold-gilded framed painting would instead showcase a screaming baby and a mother with a furrowed brow that would later need Botox.

After a few fruitless hours in the hospital, trying to get the wee babe to latch on, I buzzed the on-call hospital lactation consultant.

"Hello, I'm Mary," she announced with a thick Iranian accent when she walked into my room. "How are you, Mom?" She made a beeline toward my "girls" without ever looking at my face. She never called me by my name, always just Mom.

"Now the first one is dinner, Mom. The second is dessert." Then she grabbed my breast, reminding me that it looked like a bulls eye to help the baby latch on properly.

I darted a wide-eyed glance at Dave, who stood in a corner with his hand over his mouth, trying not to laugh.

Back home, I started to discover my new normal. For some reason, before the baby was born, I naively thought once pregnancy was over and the baby was out, I would get my body back. Oh, it might take a few weeks to fully recover, but surely my life would return to semi-normal.

Little did I realize that the day the baby arrived was the day I became a milkmaid. A full-time 24/7 nursing machine. And my body? As Scarlett O' Hara said, "I can't think about that right now. If I do, I'll go crazy. I'll think about that tomorrow."

This was my new life. All I did, day and night, was change diapers and nurse, nurse, nurse. I nursed every three hours, no matter what the hour. At first the pain was excruciating. I felt like I was on fire each time I nursed. I remember looking at Dave as tears of pain dripped off my cheeks. He sighed with sympathy. "Honey, I am so sorry. I would love to help you. But I just don't have the right equipment."

When my milk finally came in a few days after we returned home, I woke up lying on soaked sheets. At first, I had no idea what had happened. When it dawned on me that I had leaked all over the bed, I shrieked in disgust, "Aw, sick!" I wanted to melt in horror in front of my husband. Who cares about your new Pamela Anderson bra size? How can you feel sexy when you literally wet your bed in breast milk?

And it wasn't just at night. Oh no. During the day I stuffed sexy white nursing pads into my bra to absorb leakage so I wouldn't terrify Target store patrons with two wet circles in the very worst spots. One day, Dave and I pulled up to valet our car at a posh Dallas hotel for a business event. Dave walked around the car to take my hand, then yelled in horror, staring at my chest, "Leah!"

I looked down. There was the Mississippi river on one side of my beautiful, brand new yellow dress. I smashed my arm against the spot to dam the river, and Dave acted like a bodyguard shield as I made a beeline for the bathroom. Oh, nursing, it's so nice to meet you!

I distinctly remember yelling at Dave one particular day during the first few weeks. He was sitting in his home office dressed like a swanky GQ cover boy with no spit up on his starched dress shirt. I stumbled into his office in a dirty nursing tank I had slept in the night before and black sweat pants, with my greasy hair pulled back in a plastic hair clip and no make-up to cover the bags under my eyes. Dave patiently listened to my sleepless-zombie over-emotional rant of the woes of new motherhood for a good twenty minutes.

But even patient Dave has a limit. Finally, he dropped his forehead into his hand and whispered words that made my new mom blood boil: "I just don't get why it's so hard."

I reeled back like a crazed, red-eyed animal, shaking my finger at him. "What did you say? Don't you *ever* undermine what I do each day! Look, I don't even know who I am anymore! I am a professional milkmaid 24/7, 365 days a year! I can't go anywhere because I'm back nursing every two and a half hours. All I do is change diapers and take care of a baby! I have completely lost my identity! I'm just a mom *all* day and *all* night. I feel like a rat running on a wheel, and I can't jump off!"

I ran off, crying. (Dave, I am so sorry I was such a mess!) As soon as I landed on my bed, the baby started crying again. Oh, motherhood, you delightful beast.

I needed to get out of the house, but I was scared to

nurse in public. Finally, I decided to take my chances and try. My nursing friends suggested a movie theater—the perfect location to learn. I purposely choose a movie that had been out for a while and was showing on a weekday afternoon. Surely no one else would be there. I started sweating as soon as we entered the theater, terrified of causing a scene.

"The back," I whispered to Dave. "The *very* back row!" I wedged myself into my seat with Samson on my lap, and I shoved the diaper bag next to my seat for added privacy. Dave then plopped down in the chair beside me. Unfortunately, more and more patrons marched in like an entire ant colony. Finally, a grandpa and grandson were forced to sit right next to me. Oh, brother.

Halfway through the movie, Samson started fussing for milk. *I can do this, I can do this, I can do this,* I told myself. *It's normal. It's legal. It's natural.*

The movie was blaring and the house lights were out. It was the perfect time. I slowly pulled out my brand new black and white paisley nursing cover. With my eyes glued to the screen, hoping no one would notice me, I started to gingerly and then frantically find and unsnap everything underneath the foreign nursing cover while hungry Samson cried louder and louder. (I felt like that little kid who believes if he covers his eyes, no one can see him. I kept my eyes firmly on the movie screen praying no one would look back at me.) Finally, glorious silence—he'd latched on.

But unfortunately, by some freak of coincidence, the movie sound went silent at that same moment. As if he was using a baby bullhorn, Samson trumpeted the loudest rhythmic sucking noises of all time. That was all you could hear in the theater: *suck, suck, suck.* I slid lower and lower in my chair, mortified. The grandpa beside me scowled like a disapproving gray-haired Grinch while Dave turned to me with raised eyebrows and whispered, "Honey! What in the world? Can you keep it down?"

I looked back at him, wide-eyed like a deer in headlights. *"There's nothing I can do!"*

Public nursing … you've gotta love it. Like carrying the screaming, starving babe into a public bathroom stall, stripping your non-nursing dress all the way off so you have to nurse completely naked while sitting on the toilet. (What *is* that sound from that stall?) Or nursing in the driver's seat of your car in a parking lot when a luxury car pulls up and out pour several businessmen who stare down through your window. (What *is* that woman doing in there?) Or my personal favorite memory: nursing on a tiny Winnie the Pooh bench with my back to gawking teenage boys at Disneyland.

Eventually, I turned to pumping milk—aka the mechanical milkmaid. My friends and I called bagged breast milk "liquid gold" because it takes so long to make and is priceless to our sanity. It provides freedom for nursing mothers, allowing a break for a little longer than a few hours. Once you pump these bags of gold, you mark the date and ounces on the outside with a Sharpie and then shove them in the freezer. Hungry for a late night snack? Mmm, nothing more appetizing than shifting around bags of frozen breast milk to get to the chocolate ice cream.

If Dave ever tried to come in the room while I was pumping, I shrieked in horror, "No! Don't come in!" I was sure the image of me pumping breast milk would stop him from ever making a move on me again. And that sound, that horrible eerie screechy rhythmic sound: *ER-er, ER-er, ER-er.*

But, alas, one time Dave accidently walked in on me. "Get out!" I screamed so wildly that he scampered away like a man on fire. I didn't care. There was no way on earth I was ever going to let my lover see me holding two squawking plastic suction cones on my body like a trained Wisconsin dairy cow.

I nursed every three hours around the clock. Talk about zombie living. When you are habitually tired, *everything* is a BIG deal. Everything annoys you. I remember Dave walking in on me as I was nursing. If I could have taken my eyes off myself, I would have noticed his eyes were bloodshot, too.

"Honey," he began, graciously keeping his eyes on the ground so his words were less pointed. "I think it would be really beneficial if we really extended a lot of grace toward each other, because we are both really tired right now."

I burst into tears, sobbing that I was the worst wife and he was the best husband. We hugged ... until Samson wanted "dessert."

But those forced moments of nursing were often exactly what I needed in this hectic new world of parenthood. At social events, I sneaked away to a back room and took a breather with my precious little baby. All the world's worries and all the cares in my life melted away. There we were, just my baby and me. A little slice of heaven on earth. I wouldn't have traded those moments for anything.

Stop and Smell: Feeding young children—whether it's nursing, bottle feeding or making the grouchy toddler eat—can feel mundane. Try to change your perspective the next time you feed your little darling; someday you will eat your meals alone. The days of bottle feeding and nursing go fast. Try to savor these quiet "feeding" moments. They are a delicious, silent respite from the busy outside world.

Stop and Reflect:

1. If you nursed, what were some of the most positive moments? Do you recall any humorous nursing moments?

2. If you used formula, what were some funny

moments that happened in Bottleland? (I used formula, too!) If you've decided formula is the best way for you, how and why did you arrive at this decision?

3. What are some fond memories you currently have or had of nursing or bottle-feeding your baby?

4. If you are pregnant, are you contemplating nursing or using formula, or a combination? How will you decide what is best for your baby?

CHAPTER SEVEN

Oh, Baby

"A hundred years from now, it will not matter what my bank account was, the sort of house I lived in, or the kind of car I drove, but the world may be different because I was important in the life of a child."

—Forest Witcraft

The first year of parenthood felt like I'd been thrown into the deep end of a pool to figure out how to swim by myself. At first I thought I was going to drown. Every activity was new and awkward, from diapering to bathing. But after a while, I began to develop my own stroke and swim on my own in these crazy new parenting waters.

During my first week of parenting, I remember thinking, naively, *If only I can make it to the weekend.* Then the weekend hit and … nothing changed! This was our new normal.

Dave and I bought a few packages of pacifiers "just in case" we might need them when we brought our first baby home, but we just knew Samson wouldn't need any sleep props. After all, we were the perfect first-time parents; we had attended newborn parenting classes and *knew* not to create sleep aids. But that first night home from the hospital, we ripped open every package of pacifiers we had like crazed, sleepless zombies. *Anything* to let us sleep just a little longer.

Sleep deprivation felt like Chinese water torture—where the bad guys slowly dripped water on the restrained victim's forehead to drive that person insane. That's what lack of sleep felt like to me. Every time I fell asleep, it seemed like the baby started crying again.

(You know you're a sleep-deprived new mom when you tell a group of your friends about that time you traveled to New York City to see the Eiffel Tower.)

One especially hard night, after multiple wake-up-screaming episodes, Dave fell into bed, staring at the ceiling. "You know what I'm going to do? When Samson is a teenager in a dead sleep at four a.m., I am going to burst in his room crying as loud as I can to get him back for all this."

Without hesitation, I replied, "I'll do it with you!"

The first time we gave Samson a bath, we broke the one and only cardinal rule of newborn bathing. "Dave!" I cried out halfway through the bath. "We got his umbilical cord stump wet!" I felt like the worst parent in the world, madly dabbing the water droplets from his tiny belly with a washcloth.

After that I was more careful, and soon I loved bathing my new baby. He was happy and calm, staring at me when the water hit his skin. His big blue eyes seemed to ask, "Is it okay?" My mom taught me to lay a warm wet washcloth on his chest while I bathed him, so he wouldn't be scared.

I learned another bath lesson: no nestling the naked cherub in his cute hooded towel post bath. The first time I tried, overcome by my adorable naked, fresh-smelling baby, I wrapped him up in his new frog towel and sat down to rock him in the nursery. Suddenly, I felt that horrible warm, wet feeling that parents know too well. "Aw, *gross!*" I yelled to Dave downstairs. "Samson just totally peed all over me!"

Why do babies spit up on you right after you take a nice shower and feel like a normal person again? Or right before you leave the house? Or right after you put on a clean shirt? And why, when you look away from your baby boy one time when changing him, does he soak you, no matter how quickly you try to slap a diaper over the yellow fountain? My friend recommended buying Pee-pee Teepees—washable tiny cones to cover that precious little fire hose.

Dave and I kept "score" of dirty diapers according to the wipe usage. One day, he popped into the kitchen to toss a soiled diaper in the trashcan. "Honey, that was a fifteen-wiper," he said. I gasped, "Whoa, babe! Respect! You rock!"

Next on our list of firsts was going out for the first time as a family. Once I got the hang of nursing (sort of), I decided it was time to leave the house. When you travel anywhere with a newborn, you continually tote around a HUGE diaper bag and bulky infant car seat that only grows heavier as the baby gets bigger. I felt like a pack mule everywhere I went. One week into parenthood, I retired my lovely, feminine leather handbag and tossed my wallet into my practical, spill-proof diaper bag. I shuddered. What had happened to me? I felt like I was an official mom. All I needed was a minivan.

I'll never forget the day I wore heels post-pregnancy. I felt like a woman again! But clothes? Dave overheard me in my closet mumbling about how nothing fit right anymore, and logically suggested I simply buy new ones. I burst out crying. "I don't *want* to buy new clothes! I want to wear my *old* clothes!"

(Freebie for the new mama: pregnancy, nursing and post-baby body can sometimes make you feel unattractive, even if your husband reassures you of the opposite. *You* know how you used to look, and now you may feel quite different with a pregnant belly, post-baby belly pooch or wider hips. But guess what? No one can change the way you feel about yourself—

except you! I found myself sulking and complaining to Dave about my new-mom body and curves too often. Then one day I realized that I needed to quit bemoaning my changed looks. I just needed to believe I was beautiful and attractive to Dave. That made all the difference in the world. Remember, you are now a mother and you are beautiful!)

As a new mom, I sometimes just wanted things to be "normal" again. Little by little, though, I started to realize that life would never go back to "normal"—this was our new normal. On some days I didn't feel like taking care of a baby. I just wanted a long, hot, uninterrupted shower and one glorious full night of sleep. But newborn parenthood is forced selflessness. You have a child who you need to continue caring for whether you feel like it or not. There's no time off and no sick days.

Finally, after we felt like we had baby care under control and Samson started sleeping long stretches at night, we faced a new terror. The Morning Sickness Monster had spawned an evil cousin: the Teething Monster. (Teething is such a mean trick after you finally get your baby sleeping at night—now the baby is again waking up all during the night!)

The first time Samson experienced teething pains, it scared Dave and I to death. In the dead of night, Samson let out a blood-curdling scream followed by inconsolable crying. Dave and I leaped out of bed, thinking something awful had happened to our baby. Then we noticed his red gums and a tooth pushing through. The next day, I googled teething and was horrified to learn that teething pains can hurt worse than an adult toothache. Poor baby!

My *au natural* friends suggested amber bead necklaces for relief, but my man's-man Dave wasn't hot about his son wearing a necklace. So we developed a new strategy. When he cried out in the night, we laid him on his changing table and like half-asleep novice dentists, crudely rubbed teething gel on his pain-filled red gums. One rough evening, exhausted Dave peered over my shoulder as I battled to wedge my finger into Samson's screaming mouth. "More! More!" he breathed like a vampire. "Put *lots* of it on there!"

We somehow survived teething and soon discovered a terrific new stage—age six months. A whole new world unfolded. (Right after Samson was born, someone told me, "If you think having a newborn is fun, just wait until they are a little older. It's even better." And they were right!) Samson wasn't just a docile baby anymore. He was responding and interacting with me—my little buddy!

One of my favorite times of day was our naptime routine. I laid him in his crib and lifted his fuzzy blue blanket to place it over him. Samson smiled and immediately shot up all four of his limbs to catch the falling blanket. Is there anything more precious than tucking your little ones in, praying over them and reminding them how much you love them? I loved rocking Samson and singing the same songs my mother had sung over me. And what about kissing those chubby cherub cheeks? I don't think you can ever kiss your baby too much.

There's another upside to all the changing and growing. You get to buy your baby an entire new wardrobe every three months! It's a shopaholic's dream-come-true! But poor mothers of boys. There are racks and racks of baby girl clothes, but only a tiny section for the man babies.

I remember the day I put away Samson's newborn clothes and replaced them with the next size: zero-to-three months then three-to-six-month tops and pants. I decided that day to purposely revel in him each time I bought bigger clothes, knowing that I was closing another chapter of his life and ushering in a new one. (And I still do. Each time I buy new clothes for my children, I kiss them a little more and hug them a little longer.)

When Samson turned a year old, we celebrated with a lion-themed birthday party. I took a zillion pictures at the party, and the following week I sat down to add them to his first-year baby album. I will never forget that moment as I reviewed the album in dismay. Wait! What in the world had happened? The ratio of baby-and-mom pictures to baby-and-dad pictures was 1:2,094. (Who's with me on this? Ladies, take some photos of your mama friends with their babies. Let's balance this ratio!)

Food became a new adventure. One time, I gave Samson a piece of bread to feed the ducks in the nearby park. Instead of feeding the ducks he ate the whole slice while watching me feed the rest of the loaf to the ducks. Another time I discovered Samson stuffing his mouth full of dog food right alongside our dog, Princess. "Spit it out, Samson!" I demanded with my hand cupped under his chin. He finally relented. Then, with tears still streaming down his cheeks, he defiantly jammed the dog food he was saving in his little fists into his mouth—right in front of me. Maybe we went a little overboard on the no dog-food-eating training. Soon after I discovered him yelling, "No! No! No!" at Princess as she attempted to eat her own dog food. Poor dog.

And there were other new adventures. One time, I found that Samson had dunked *one hundred paper napkins* in the toilet and then plopped them individually all over the kitchen floor. A few weeks later, I found him stomping 192 individual-serving-size containers of International Delight coffee creamer all over the floor, stopping only to lick up the popped ones. Another time, I found the saltshaker completely emptied all over the table, right beside a bowl filled with fruit that had one tiny bite taken out of every piece. Later on, I found him and his entire bedroom cloaked in a cloud of white—he had discovered the economy-size bottle of baby powder.

But all of these experiences paled in comparison to his favorite activity: unrolling every toilet paper roll in the house. Every time we—or our poor guests—went into a bathroom, there was a big, snowy pile of toilet paper heaped below the empty cardboard roll.

Stop and Smell: Sometimes when your little one is crying or fussing, strangers ask, "What's wrong with your baby?" My mom told me she often answered with, "Oh, he/she must be teething." She used that answer whether we had no teeth or all our teeth because it made her feel better to have some sort of explanation as a newbie parent. I used it, too. For example, one time Samson, at about four years of age, had a grocery store meltdown. I turned to Dave and said, "Ah, he must be teething." Dave nodded back. "Oh, definitely." Have fun not knowing all the answers as new parents!

Stop and Reflect:

1. What are some of the misconceptions you had about being a parent?

2. What are some of the things that turned out just as you expected?

3. What are some of the sweet moments you've shared with your new baby?

4. If you're pregnant, what are some things you are looking forward to doing with your new baby?

CHAPTER EIGHT

The Day It All Changed

"No farewell words were spoken, no time to say goodbye.
You were gone before we knew it, and only God knows why."

—Anonymous

"I'm pregnant!" I shrieked, out of breath from running upstairs with a positive pregnancy test. "We're going to have another baby!"

I pounced on my husband's sleeping form at 7 a.m. on a Monday morning. After a few quick questions, we shared ecstatic grins and then joyful silence as the news sank in for both of us. Holding me in his arms as we lay in bed, Dave offered a prayer: "Lord, we dedicate this child to you for as long as you see fit. Thank you for this baby."

The next day was a blur of happiness. Would it be a boy or girl? Due in November, only sixteen months after Samson's birth, it would be almost like having twins! Despite being pregnant through another Texas summer, we would have TWO children! We would need a bigger house! A minivan! Another crib!

How were we going to tell everyone? I printed an "I'm going to be a Big Brother!" shirt for Samson. I chatted on the phone with my pregnant girlfriends, rejoicing in how close in age all of our children would be. Life couldn't be any sweeter.

I was ten weeks along when Dave and I went to our first doctor appointment. As with my first pregnancy, I was nauseated and vomiting. I lay still while the doctor squirted cold jelly on my stomach and ... *wham!* There was my womb on the big flat-screen mounted on the wall.

"Twins?" I joked, half hoping.

The doctor smiled as we all stared at the beautiful baby on the sonogram screen. "No twins this time. Just one baby." The doctor moved the wand slowly, and the image became clearer.

I then remembered Samson's eight-week sonogram and the flickering light indicating his heartbeat. After some time, I asked, "Where's the heartbeat?"

"Well, it's early to see it. That's why I usually suggest an internal sonogram this early along." The doctor paused for a moment. "When was the last time you felt nauseated?"

"Today. Right now."

The internal sonogram showed the baby at the bottom of my uterus, completely still. The doctor cranked up the volume, straining to hear a heartbeat. After a few horrific seconds of monotone static, instead of a reassuring *thud, thud, thud,* I tore my eyes away from the screen. I didn't want to look at a lifeless baby.

The doctor excused himself to get another physician to confirm the "missed miscarriage," a term I never knew before that day. It meant that my baby's heart had stopped beating, but my body had "missed" that the baby was no longer alive and was attempting to sustain the pregnancy.

While we waited alone in the sonogram room for the second doctor to come in, Dave reminded me that we had dedicated this child to the Lord for as long as he saw fit. "It's the Lord's child," he said. "We're just stewards."

I nodded blankly.

A second doctor briskly swept in. "Hi, Mr. and Mrs. Spina. I'm sorry to meet you under these circumstances."

I looked away again, feeling even sicker as I stared at my belly while the doctor moved the wand around and examined the baby on the screen. The doctors then gave me three options: Opt for a D and C (dilation and curettage) surgery to remove the fetus, take pills to induce labor or wait up to four weeks to see if my body would respond and naturally pass the baby. I told the doctor we would wait.

Heavy with grief, Dave and I walked out of the sonogram room and back to the waiting room to leave. Just as we opened the door to exit, the receptionist called out, "Mrs. Spina, would you like to make your next appointment?"

I blankly stared at her, then realized she had no idea what we had just learned. "I'll call you," I mumbled.

We got on the elevator with a mother and her three beautiful living children, and I smashed my back against the elevator wall. As we walked outside hand in hand, Dave reminded me—and probably himself as well—that God is good, but we live in a fallen world. I just wanted my baby.

Three weeks later I miscarried.

During this time, I learned a life-changing lesson. Sorrow can breed joy. Loss can breed gratitude. My miscarriage made me feel like the air had been knocked out of me, like I was no longer able to breathe. But I eventually started breathing life again. Big, deep gulps of air, like those of a drowning person emerging from a deep, dark sea. I would never *ever* take children or parenthood for granted again.

Stop and Smell: Losing a child is like pledging a sorority no one wants to join. But the beautiful fruit can be gratitude. Now, when I host baby showers, I always stop to remind the guests that God is the Giver of life and a new baby is something we should never take for granted. Mamas, hug your babies a little closer today.

Stop and Reflect:

1. By the time we reach adulthood, most of us have lost someone very special to us. How has loss affected you?

2. Do you fear something happening to your child? How do you combat those fears?

3. Stories of loss propel us to cherish our little ones. How can you stop to cherish your child today?

CHAPTER NINE

Extraordinary Ordinary Moments

"What day is it?'
'It's today,' squeaked Piglet.
'My favorite day,' said Pooh.''

–A.A. Milne

After my miscarriage, I transformed into a completely different mother. Each day of routine motherhood was like my own personal Disneyland of thrills. From the moment I woke up, I searched for and reveled in the tiny magical moments of parenthood. I let the house go to experience the little joys of each moment. I left projects uncompleted to catch them. Each day with my child became a gift to savor. Here are just a few of the extraordinary ordinary experiences I've relished over the past four years and what I've learned from them.

* * *

"Mama! Watch cars!" chirped Samson.

I looked down at my little boy as we walked toward the doors of the post office, wondering what he meant. Soon I realized he wanted me to sit on the curb beside him and watch the cars drive by on the busy adjacent street. Even though my hands were full of heavy packages, I plopped down beside him. Just a tiny toddler and a thirty-something mom sitting quietly on a public concrete curb watching cars drive by. We do it often now, even in quiet parking lots with long waits between cars.

I once sheepishly tried to explain to curious onlookers, "Uh, we're just watching the cars," but no one understood. So now we shamelessly sit with our bags around us as we watch the cars while people stare at us and wonder.

Stopping to "just be" with my small children was hard for me at first. Is it easy or hard for you?

* * *

We flew down to Corpus Christi, Texas, for a family vacation. After a long day, I decided to spend some fun time with Samson. I drove our Suburban onto the deserted beach on a weeknight, 5:30 p.m. Then I lifted Samson out of his car seat onto the Texas "snow." The evening wind kicked up and tousled his overgrown mop of white hair. He looked so cute in just his Batman swimsuit.

We trotted across the sand, burning energy before bedtime. Suddenly, I yelled, "Samboy! Look! You're making tracks!"

He spun around to examine his tiny footprints in the sand. Without a word he was off, running as fast as his tanned little feet could go. Every seven steps or so, he peeked over his shoulder to examine the magically appearing footprints. Finally, after a solid ten minutes of running in random patterns, he stopped, panting. "Look ... at my tracks ... Mama! Look at my ... tracks!"

I soaked in the sight of his scrawny arms hanging at his side and his naked toddler potbelly, heaving in and out above his swimsuit. I imagined him in a few fast years, tall and lanky, looking down at me instead of me looking down at him. "What?" I yelled in a mock-stern voice. "I'm a policeman, and you just made tracks on my beach! I'm gonna get you!"

We were off again, me chasing a squealing boy who finally collapsed in giggles and tickles on the sand. Oh, time be still, I thought. I'm playing with my boy and I never want this to end.

Do you joke around with your child? The magical part of young-child humor is they laugh at just about any stab at humor, even the silliest joke. You are the best Saturday Night Live comedian in your child's eyes! Just go for it!

* * *

When Dave and I were dating, we did something cheeseball. While holding hands, we squeezed three times to signify the words "I love you." It was our secret code that we could use anytime or anywhere without anyone knowing.

One day when Samboy and I were crossing a parking lot, I taught him this code. I cannot tell you how precious it is every time he initiates it when we are holding hands, which is a lot since he is still young. He squeezes as tight as he can and sometimes gets the number of squeezes wrong, but his smile up at me afterward is a mental picture that I will treasure to my old age.

I love watching parents shower affection and words of kindness on their children. Isn't it amazing that we are their very first examples of compassion, love and kindness?

* * *

Sometimes a moment happens that is so precious, I want to remember it for the rest of my life! At my brother's wedding, I was sitting there in my billowy taupe bridesmaid dress when Samson, age two, ran up to me in his tiny black and white tuxedo. He grabbed my hand and chirped, "Dance with me, Mama? Dance with me?"

He pulled me onto the hardwood dance floor and grabbed both of my hands, looking up at me while swaying. I realized that someday we would dance again, maybe on his wedding day when he would be a man in a tuxedo looking down at me instead of me looking down at me. But today I gazed at my darling in ecstatic joy. Then it hit me that even though my baby would grow into a boy who would grow into a man, I would *always* be his mother.

What kind of in-law do you think you'll be? I don't know about you, but I find myself already looking for my children's potential spouses! Can you believe that? But, hey, it sure would be nice if they married some of our best friends' children, right? You thought I was just setting up a playdate? I'm really matchmaking toddlers.

* * *

How in the world can I say no, despite how tired I am, when Samson runs up to me with his Batman mask squishing his nose so tight that it sounds like he has a stuffed nose and says, "Mama, you be da Joker?"

Of course I will be da Joker. Of course.

It's so hard to play with toddlers when you are tired. And sometimes I don't. But when I do make the effort, I always find that it's a day well spent. We're only parents once, and we only get this day one time.

* * *

I'll never forget the day Samson used a vending machine for the first time in his life. At the library, a kind older gentlemen had presented him with a dollar bill to buy a snack. I helped him push the correct numbers with his tiny index finger, then turned to tend to his whining sister.

"Mom! How do we get it?" he asked.

I looked down at my little boy, realizing he had never used a vending machine before. (I always want to stop and savor these firsts with my children!) "Oh! Sorry, buddy! Right here. Push that special door back. It's like a giant robot spitting out the food you want."

We walked out through the automatic glass doors with Samson chomping on his first vending machine snack. As I pushed the stroller across the parking lot, I thought about the older gentleman's kindness to a mama struggling in a library line with two squiggly young children, a stroller and a bag full of heavy picture books. I think I'll hand out one-dollar bills to overwhelmed mamas at my local library, when I am a granny.

What have you enjoyed watching your child experience the first time?

Stop and Smell: "Parent like a grandparent," a friend once told me. If a child is missing a sock when he or she jumps in the car for an ice cream trip, grandparents don't sweat it. They're so happy to just be with their grandkids and make fun memories that they could care less about a silly missing sock. Grandparents are getting a second chance at parenting, and they're often all the wiser in their perspective. They see the big picture, love a lot more, and care a lot less about the unimportant details that stress new parents. For them, it's just not that big of a deal. And, if you really think about it, they are right.

Stop and Reflect:

1. What is one of your own favorite memories from early parenting days?

2. Is it easy or difficult for you to "be in the moment" when parenting your young children? Why?

3. If you are pregnant, do you think it will easy or challenging for you to discover extraordinary parenting moments as a new mom?

CHAPTER TEN

Another Baby

"Having a baby is a life changer.

It gives you a whole other perspective on why you wake up every day."

–Taylor Hanson

A year after the miscarriage, we were pregnant again. But this pregnancy was not magical. A week after discovering the good news, Dave and I drove down to a small Texas town for a friend's wedding. We stayed at a restored, historic hotel from the 1930s with tiny rooms and gold-gilded ceilings.

The morning after the wedding, we packed up and I went to the bathroom before our road trip home. After discovering a small amount of blood, I stumbled out of the bathroom to lie down on the bed. I felt like I was about to faint. A wave of terror swept over me as I remembered my miscarriage starting the same way. Strong, steady, painful contractions began. I just knew I was losing this baby, too.

I lay on the back seat for the entire drive home, breathing slowly as tears streamed down my face. *Why God?* I silently asked. *Why this again? What is the purpose?* At each stop, and at each bathroom, there was more spotting.

The contractions and spotting waned after a few days

but left me terrified. Every time I went to the bathroom, I wondered if I would find blood. I wanted to conquer my fear and hated living in constant dread of the future and the what-ifs. I tried to stifle negative thoughts and surround myself with truth, but fears lurked everywhere.

At twelve weeks, right around the time of my previous miscarriage, I started contracting hard. This time the contractions didn't stop but grew more intense. After forty-eight hours, we called my OB/GYN and scheduled an appointment. Our amazing, optimistic doctor walked into the room and greeted us with firm handshakes. He then looked me right in my eye and said, "Okay, let's hear that heartbeat loud and clear."

As he slid the wand over my stomach in silence, searching for a heartbeat sound, I held my breath. Then we all heard the glorious *bump, bump, bump.*

I burst into tears, jarring the transducer with my compulsive sobs. "It's alive! It's alive! Oh, thank you, doctor!" I was embarrassed to cry so hard in front of the doctor and nurse, but once you've tasted loss, you never forget it.

(By the way, I have a question about OB/GYN exam rooms. Does that glossy beach scene photo ripped from a magazine and crudely Scotch-taped on the ceiling above the exam table help *anyone* calm down when they are about to be checked? Anyone?)

I was a different mom this time around, full of gratitude. I loved morning sickness. I reveled in the vomiting and constant nausea. It confirmed that the baby was growing and doing well! How could I complain about anything when the best gift ever—a baby—was growing inside of me? But it was hard to think of it as *my* baby. I was ecstatic to be pregnant, but I kept my emotional connection at bay so I wouldn't get hurt if we lost this child, too.

I dreaded the routine prenatal appointments. I wanted to ball up in a dark hole until the baby was born, away from any potential bad news or tests. I was terrified they would find something wrong again. Soon after I started to feel the baby move—oh, glorious moving alive baby—I grew scared and shaky on my way to the doctor's office. Would the baby be still alive for this visit? What would we find at this check-up? At each stop light, I held the wheel with one hand and pushed on my pregnant belly with the other until the baby moved. *Thank God the baby is still alive!* I thought.

At the office, I scribbled my name on the sign-in sheet, then sat in a blue chair surrounded by a sea of other pregnant women. I felt very different from them. They probably had never miscarried and looked forward to these checkups, like I had when I was pregnant Pollyanna with Samson. As the nurse called out names, the women rose with a smile and waddled to the door while I continued to push on my stomach to encourage movement.

I didn't want to tell anyone other than family that I was pregnant until after the big twenty-week sonogram, when they extensively examine the baby to ensure major organs and body systems have developed correctly. On the day of that appointment, the memories of the horrific sonogram that showed our lifeless baby haunted me. My hands shook as I pulled on pregnancy jeans, a sparkly grey maternity T-shirt and slipped into silver snakeskin flats. Dave cancelled his work so he could come with me.

My mouth felt dry as the technician walked us back to the sonogram room. She gave me instructions, and I mechanically undressed and laid down on the exam table. The tech returned and turned off the light. Dave held my hand as she squirted the cold jelly on my belly and pressed the wand into the middle of it. I stared at Dave's face, not the screen. She glided the wand around and rattled off routine check-up comments.

Finally, unable to breathe, I whispered, "Does everything look okay?"

She nodded without taking her eyes off the screen. "Everything looks just fine, Mrs. Spina."

Dave joyfully squeezed my ice-cold hand while silent grateful tears slid down my cheeks. Only then did I look up at the image of the baby. It was moving. There was the beautiful white flickering heartbeat. Throughout my future sonograms, I could not look at the screen until the technician or doctor said everything looked fine.

When we finished the sonogram, the tech left and I dressed with trembling hands and a smile no one could rip off my face. The nurse led us through a maze of hallways back to the waiting room. I wanted to shout out to each passing person, "The baby is okay! The baby is alive! The baby is normal!" Never *ever* again would I take a routine everything-looks-okay prenatal visit for granted. To this day, when someone sends me a pregnancy update after a sonogram or routine prenatal visit, I rejoice as if they've won the presidency.

When I passed through the same waiting room on my way out, I wondered if any of the waiting patients could be as happy as I was to receive a normal everything-looks-good report. I felt like doing ten cartwheels outside the office door.

Yes, sorrow had bred fear. But never had I tasted such joy.

Stop and Smell: Suffering changes us. It's how we respond that determines the type of change. Some people grow bitter, comparing their lot with others who have never tasted their harsh circumstance. Others mourn and then grow and blossom into a beautiful new person full of depth, empathy and compassion. My mother told me that when we experience suffering, we gain a new ministry for others experiencing the same type of suffering. I never wanted a "miscarriage ministry," but I can now comfort others in the same way that kind miscarriage-sufferers comforted me. If you have lost a child, I encourage you to find healing through supporting others in their loss.

"Now if we are afflicted, it is for your consolation and salvation, which is effective for enduring the same sufferings which we also suffer." 2 Corinthians 1:4 NKJV

Stop and Reflect:

1. How were your first and second pregnancies different or the same?

2. How did you feel when you knew you were going to have another child?

3. How did you find out you were pregnant again, and what was your spouse's reaction?

4. You may want to write this story down. Your second child might like to hear it someday, and you'll want to remember it, too!

5. If you have one child, what are some of your favorite ways to spend time with your child?

6. If you are pregnant, how do you feel about your prenatal appointments? Do you enjoy them? Why or why not?

CHAPTER ELEVEN

Pregnancy Plus A Toddler

"Parenting is not for sissies. You have to sacrifice and grow up."

–Jillian Michaels

Gone were the golden days of pregnancy napping whenever I was tired. A bouncing little boy with more energy than a high school cheerleader now demanded my zapped energy.

(You know you're exhausted in the toddler-plus-pregnancy season when you wake up in the morning dressed in your clothes from the day before. Putting on PJs? Too tired.)

During my worst bouts of morning sickness, I strapped poor Samson into his high chair in front of the TV with the food I thought would distract him the longest. Then I would collapse onto the couch next to him until he would get bored and cry to be let out. Samson, however, thought morning sickness was awesome. When I vomited, he laughed his head off and then fake vomited into the toilet from his place right beside me.

As a pregnant mother of a toddler, I started to do things I'd never done before, because I was exhausted and desperate. I wiped my kid's snotty nose with my bare hand. I used the grapes-of-wrath strategy in the grocery store—I stuffed a bag of red grapes next to Samson in the cart to keep him occupied while we shopped. You could follow our exact route through the store using the smashed grape trail. At home, I kicked all his toys into a pile and ordered him to put them away *or else*. I certainly couldn't bend over to pick them up.

With my second child, I wasn't scared of labor and delivery. In fact, I was looking forward to it. Two nights in a hospital that treated me like a queen, grandparents babysitting the high-energy toddler, nurses to take care of the baby, and 24/7 room service. The hospital was the seasoned mom's Ritz.

Wary of a repeat, unending-labor-and-delivery saga, we opted for a hospital birth but decided to try the no-drug delivery yet again. My *au natural* friends promised it would be "much faster" and "much easier" the second time around since my body would know what to do since it had done it before. *Is there any science to prove any of this?* I wondered. I was too busy vomiting my eyeballs out to research it.

I was ecstatic that we were having another child. I told Dave many nights, "I just can't believe God is going to let us do it all over again!" But then one morning I realized that after the baby was born, it would never be just Samson and me ever again. I looked over at my little guy eating a banana in his high chair. What was about to happen to this life I loved?

From that day on, I made an effort to stop and appreciate my time with my white-haired darling. I took him on little dates every chance I could before the baby arrived. We went to the park to feed the ducks, took long neighborhood walks and read picture books until my voice went hoarse. He was my tiny companion during mundane errands, my minute comrade at dusk on the front lawn, and my chatterbox in the back seat when I was driving. *Can I possibly love another child like I love Samson?* I asked myself.

Then came the dilemma of bumping Samson out of his crib and into a new room so the baby could have the nursery. Guilt haunted me at every step. Would he feel displaced by the new baby? Dave and I went to great lengths to create a new bedroom in a Lightning McQueen theme from the animated movie *Cars*, Samson's favorite at the time. I sewed curtains from black-and-white-checked material on my sewing machine. Dave carefully smoothed gigantic Cars character decals that I special ordered on the Internet on the walls. We both almost went cross-eyed late one night as we tried to flatten racing stickers on his new red plastic car bed to make it look like Lightning McQueen.

I was terribly nervous the night we brought him in to see his new room. I was pregnant, emotional and couldn't handle the thought of Samson crying over getting kicked out of his old room to make room for the baby. "Samboy," I said. "Come see your new big-boy room!"

Samson's reaction melted my fears. His jaw dropped with a gasp, his little blue eyes soaked up the room in a slow three-hundred-sixty-degree scan, and then he pointed to and identified each Cars character on the wall. "Look, Mama!" he squealed. "It's Mater!"

I squatted down, as best I could with a gigantic belly, and hugged his little neck. "So you like it, honey? Remember, when the baby comes, this is *your* special room. And I will always love you, sweet boy, no matter what happens. You know that, right?"

Unlike the hours of preparation for the arrival of our first child, our second baby preparation was almost an afterthought. "Honey," I said, one night only a week before my due date, as I sprawled on our couch like an obese orangutan. "So I guess I'll just reuse all the nursery bedding from Samson since it's gender neutral? I suppose the baby can use Samson's old infant car seat, and the diaper bag is still in good condition.

But I should get something together for the hospital, too."

I threw together a bag with three yellow onesies and a blanket. Poor second child!

Stop and Smell: You can't slam on the brakes in parenthood. Your child continues to grow and change, no matter how much you want to hit a "pause" button on the current season. But we can enjoy each season! Here's an idea. Use passages of time—birthdays, holidays, the four seasons, etc.—to stop and enjoy your child. Create traditions and take time to truly love on your children even in the midst of the busyness. For my childhood birthdays, my mom made waffles with faces from fruit and hung the same multi-colored happy birthday banner in the kitchen. When I grew older and could have a friend over for my birthday, Mom "hid" a raisin in the waffle batter. Whoever found it in their waffle got a dollar. Somehow it always ended up in our guest's waffle. We love to laugh about our childhood traditions as adults today. Traditions meld a strong family.

Stop and Reflect:

1. How does your family celebrate birthdays? These special days could become family traditions. They don't have to be elaborate.

2. You can also create a weekly tradition, like a movie and pizza night on Fridays. Do you have any ideas how you could create a weekly tradition to develop a fun family culture in your home?

3. How did you help your first child prepare for the arrival of a sibling? Did you ever worry that you couldn't love a second child as much as you loved your first?

4. If you're pregnant, what traditions can you think of that would create lasting memories?

CHAPTER TWELVE

Au Natural Birth

*"My friend Kathy is the only person who'll be halfway honest with me.
Did you ever see a cowboy film, where someone has been caught by the
Indians and tied between two wild stallions,
each pulling in opposite directions?' she asked.
I nodded mutely. 'That's a bit what giving birth is like.'"*

–Marian Keyes,
*Under the Duvet: Shoes, Reviews, Having the Blues, Builders, Babies,
Families and Other Calamities*

Unlike my previous *au natural* birth plan, where being induced was considered "the devil," I greedily set an induction date a week past my due date. I was a tired pregnant mama ready to have the baby as soon as possible. But I ended up going into labor on my own on a crisp March Saturday, three days past my due date.

The day I went into labor, I attended an afternoon baby shower for a friend with my mother and my pregnant sister, who was due only a month after me. At the shower, the guests nibbled chicken salad sandwiches and chocolate-covered strawberries, smiling and cooing at the pink baby girl outfits and tiny presents. I started to feel light contractions under my striped blue maternity shirt. (Tell me, why do clothes designers create horizontal-striped maternity shirts? Worst idea ever. Makes you look like an obese bumblebee.)

Soon the contractions grew so intense that I had to stop talking at times to breathe through them. I finally asked my mother to drive me home and gasped in pain at each bump or sudden stop. I yelled at my sweet mother like a hot-tempered teenager: "Mom! Quit stopping like that! It huuurts!"

Mom tried to keep a straight face. "Honey, I am driving normal."

Still doubting this could possibly be the real thing after Samson's birthing marathon, I waved good-bye to my mother from the front door and then went up to the bedroom and fell into bed exhausted and in pain. Soon I moaned out at Dave for help.

"What do you want me to do?" he asked.

I told him to take Samson to the park to feed the ducks. (I wished I could have fed ducks.)

The fierce contractions kept coming, like a mean bully dunking me under water again and again. I picked up my phone with shaking hands and tried to download an app to time the contractions before another one hit. They were timing at less than five minutes apart. It was game time. We called the doula (a natural birth coach), my chiropractor and my poor mother who had just arrived at her home an hour away.

When they all arrived, I paced back and forth like a nervous cat, worried that my contractions would die out like they did with Samson and everyone would have been troubled for nothing. I changed into a string bikini to labor in our whirlpool tub. Unbeknownst to me, my top fell off at some point, but no one told me because I was screaming in pain. Well, hello, topless screeching crazy lady! You will make a fine mama.

Gritty transition labor hit, creating the worst, most horrific pain I had ever experienced. They say that when transition hits, even sainted women sit up and swear like a sailor. I felt totally out of control and yelled to everyone that I wanted to go to the hospital *now* and get an epidural *now.* Forget the natural stuff. I climbed out of the tub and toweled off, then threw on a black T-shirt dress. I slowly made my way to the driveway, stopping to breathe through contractions.

I ripped open the passenger door to our big white Suburban, swearing inwardly that I couldn't climb in without assistance and knowing that stepping up into it would trigger another horrific contraction. *Why did Dave buy such a stupid big car?* I seethed. *And where is Dave? Doesn't he know I'm in the worst pain of my life?*

A minute later Dave burst out of the garage. "Sorry, honey," he said and smoothed a monogrammed striped beach towel on my seat, in case I leaked.

I hissed back like a python, "What? You made me wait for *this?* Who cares about your dumb car? Can't you see I'm in paaain? Start driving nooow!"

That twenty-minute bumpy ride to the hospital was a laboring mom's torture chamber. Each turn, each bump, each acceleration forced another grisly contraction. Dave drove like a soldier on a serious mission, with both hands white-knuckling the steering wheel while I howled like a coyote at each new contraction. His face flickered in the dark as street lights whizzed by while I bellowed at him, "Are you TRYING to cause pain, because YOU ARE! STOP IT!"

Without eye contact, he quipped, "Okay, I'm not even going to *try* to talk to you right now, Leah."

The baby was coming faster than any of us realized. We flew into the hospital parking lot like heroes in a good action movie scene. I prayed to God no one was there. But no, it looked like a Beatles concert had let out in the parking lot. I knew I was about to cause a scene, but I had no choice. I hit the pavement, triggering a wretched contraction. I roared through the pain like a lion at the zoo while my soft-spoken doula stroked my arm and soothed, "Reeelax." (Sorry for all the animal analogies, but I morphed into different animal sounds as I progressed in labor. Also, give me a break. I have two small children and we read a lot of animal books.)

As each contraction ended, I scrambled a few steps as fast as I could toward the glass Doors of Drugs until another one hit. Everyone gawked at the awkward trio: the trailing husband, the calming doula and the crazed blonde preggo. I could have cared less.

If you want fast service in a hospital, walk in yelling like Tarzan's cousin. The receptionist didn't ask me a single question. In five seconds flat, she grilled Dave for the basics and wheeled me away. The wheelchair contractions were horrific, like sitting on a fire. But I concentrated on the light at the end of the labor tunnel: pain relief was coming.

Finally, they carted me to my room and checked me. (My favorite part, dontcha know.) I was at nine centimeters, but my water hadn't broken. The doctor arrived within minutes. He dryly advised that it was too late for an epidural because I was so far progressed that I would deliver before it kicked in, so he would break my water, triggering harder and more painful contractions, but then the baby should come quickly.

I promptly vomited, wiped my mouth with the back of my hand to gain composure in my backless pale blue hospital gown and panted, "You have got to be kidding me. I am at a hospital and you will not give me drugs?"

Dave sent a quick text to let the family know the baby was about to be born. Our mothers jumped in a car together and drove so fast toward the hospital that a police car *tried* to pull them over for speeding. (Key word: "tried.") The police car soon turned on its lights and sirens and followed the two grandmas, but apparently new grandbabies trump the law in Grandmaland. Our mothers didn't stop and continued to speed a full additional ten minutes to the hospital parking lot.

They slid to a screeching stop in front of the hospital entrance, and my mother-in-law, the driver, yelled at my mother to go in since it was her daughter in labor. As soon as my mother exited the car, the police officer jumped out of his cruiser and fell on one knee with a loaded gun pointed at her, yelling, "Hands in the air! Hands in the air!"

My mother-in-law got a $400 ticket that I am framing in my baby book. Every time we saw a new nurse or doctor after the baby was born, he or she would give a professional introduction, then smile and say, "I just have to ask. Are you the one whose family was held at gun point in the parking lot?"

In the meantime, the doctor had broken my water and I pushed for twenty minutes *au natural*. Great balls of fire, that hurt. Finally, a beautiful black-haired baby girl popped out. I couldn't believe it was a girl and neither could Dave! When he walked down the hallway and told our waiting family that it was a girl, they screamed so loud that the nurses ran in like angry hens to remind them to keep it down and to *please* remember there were other patients. Total time for my labor and delivery was a cool six hours. No wonder it hurt so bad!

(A fellow patient later stopped me in the hospital hallway to ask if I was the one the whole hospital had heard screaming. What do you say to that? "Oh, why, yes! That was me. So nice to meet you. I see we have matching hospital gowns. I'm Leah.")

After I scarfed down two bowls of Raisin Bran cereal, I held my baby girl for the first time. After a miscarriage, there is nothing more wonderful than holding a live healthy baby. Even though I felt like I didn't deserve it, God had given me another child. Never again would I view parenthood as an ordinary adulthood experience. Children are an unbelievable gift to savor and enjoy each day.

I kissed Baby Esther's black hair, wet and fresh from her first bath, and fingered her tiny hands and feet. My man's-man Dave looked down at his two girls, smiled and said, "Well, I guess now I *really* have to learn to be more sensitive."

Stop and Smell: Getting pregnant, pregnancy, and labor and delivery can be a wild ride. Enjoy it as best as you can! As your children get older, try telling them a few stories about when they were in mommy's tummy or what they did as a baby. Samson loves having me to tell him about "Baby Samson"— how excited we were to meet him, how he used to "ride an imaginary bicycle" while watching the ceiling fan as a new baby, and how he used to destroy every toilet paper roll in the house. Not only does it bring back fun memories as a parent, but it also makes children feel wanted and loved.

Stop and Reflect:

1. What are some of the things you remember most about the birth of your child or children?

2. What things would your spouse say are the most memorable?

3. What is your favorite and least favorite part about the labor and delivery process?

4. Try writing out your second child's birth story. My mother used to tell us our birth stories on our birthdays. It was a fun tradition!

5. If you are pregnant, what are your thoughts and feelings toward labor and delivery? What are you nervous about and what are you looking forward to?

CHAPTER THIRTEEN

Bringing Home The Second Child

"A baby is God's opinion that the world should go on."

–Carl Sandburg

One of the sweetest moments after Baby Esther's birth was when Samson met his sister for the first time. He gingerly tiptoed around the hospital bed, and we presented him a wrapped present from the baby—a new toy monster truck— to warm him up. He then took a long look at his sleeping new sister. His first words were, "She has no eyes, Mama! She has no eyyyes!"

When it was time to leave the hospital, I pulled on a pink sweat suit, pink Crocs and a hot pink nursing tank. I hopped in the mandatory wheelchair, cradling a bouquet of fresh flowers and a pink "It's a Girl!" balloon. Dave trailed behind carrying Baby Esther in her masculine plaid blue car seat. (We didn't know the baby was going to be a girl—poor child!) Everyone we passed in the stark, sterile white hallway smiled and congratulated us. I felt like the queen of a glorious tiny parade, waving and nodding back. What happy times. I always want to savor moments like these instead of bulldozing on to the next event.

When we pulled up to our house, our neighbors and family stood waving on our front yard like cheery daisies in the wind. Dave's mother always makes a big deal about special occasions—she loves to celebrate and appreciate life's blessings—and Baby Esther's birth was no exception. Our front yard looked like a pink princess coronation.

A gigantic pink sign that covered our entire garage door announced "IT'S A GIRL!" to the world. A personalized pink stork sign stuck in the grass bragged her birth stats: 8 lb. 1 oz., 21 inches. A bouquet of pink and white balloons danced at the front door. Little Samboy in his Batman T-shirt ran as fast as he could downhill across the flowerbeds toward his daddy, and Dave hoisted him up to peer down at Baby Esther in her car seat. We were an official family of four.

Then Samson studied my post-baby body emerging from the car. He asked, "Gotta 'nother baby in der, Mama?" Thanks, son.

My angel mother stayed to help us for the first week after Esther's arrival. She assisted during the day, and Dave pitched in at night. When morning finally broke after a long, sleepless night, Dave stuck his head out our bedroom door and yelled, "Day shift!" My beaming mother came trotting down the hallway with a hot breakfast and a fresh flower on a tray. (Can I get an *amen* for loving family and friends who support new parents? You are amazing!)

I was more confident and relaxed this second time around. Eh, I didn't care what opinionated people thought anymore! Stern parenting advice didn't flatten me like it did before. How could I debate sleep training topics when I was just so thrilled to have a living, breathing baby? I was too busy being happy to think about anything else. After I endured the loss of a child, I emerged a different person into a different world. Sheer gratitude pushed everything else aside. This was the beginning of the rest of my life, and I wanted to stop and savor every moment until the day I died.

Stop and Smell: You may be smack dab in the middle of tough parenting, but what can you be grateful for? We must *look* for the blessings in the middle of the diaper blizzard. If not, we'll work away with blinders on our eyes until our children grow into independence. Then we'll wonder where those precious little years went. Anytime an elderly person stops you in the store to remind you, "They grow so fast," take it to heart. *Live in the now and focus on the good.*

Stop and Reflect:

1. Did you feel more confident as a parent the second time around?

2. How did your first child respond to the new baby?

3. Whether you have had one or more children, how has having a child made you a better person?

4. If you are pregnant, how do you think having a child will change you for the better?

CHAPTER FOURTEEN

The Sleepless Zombie Zone

"I'm a walking zombie and I think I'm going to be like that for a while."

–Tiffani Thiessen

There really *is* a difference between having a baby girl after a baby boy. I saw it in the way Dave immediately started calling Baby Esther "honey" and "sweetie" in the hospital, the way boisterous Samboy paused from wild monster truck play to tenderly hug her, and the way we all naturally called her "Baby Esther"—never just "Esther."

But this same darling princess also turned us into crazy people. Samson was a rock-star newborn sleeper, always on schedule. Baby Esther? She. Never. Slept. She screamed all night long between the nastiest hours of all—midnight through 4 a.m.—crying and crying and crying. All my tried and true tactics that worked like a charm with Samson went right out the door. I was desperate and tried everything. Changed the diaper. Nursed. Tried to burp. Tried a pacifier. Swaddled. Unswaddled. Rocked. Took her to bed with me. Put her to bed alone.

One night, I burst into our bedroom, my hands covering my bloodshot eyes, while Baby Esther screamed in the background. "David! You *have* to take over! I cannot handle this anymore! I don't know what is wrong with her! I've tried everything and she just keeps crying and waking up! Please! I'm scared I will shake her!"

Finally, we called in the big guns—my mother. (She has cared for over one hundred infants as a volunteer transitional care parent for a large adoption agency, caring for the newborns before they are adopted.) I burst into tears when she arrived on my doorstep. Oh, please help us, kind angel of hope! But even my mother had no magic sleep wand or lullaby tricks. Baby Esther was just a cranky baby and we'd have to wait it out. Night after night after night.

Before Baby Esther, I turned up my nose at sleep props. "Oh no. We sleep train our children." I smiled naively. "My baby will sleep anywhere, in any lighting, with any sound." Then came Baby Esther. I ran back to my friends like a dog with its tail between its legs and apologized profusely for all my sleep advice. I now knew nothing. When the sun began to sink, I inwardly whimpered like a puppy terrified of what the night would bring. I drained our bank account on custom blackout curtains, noise machine, fans and swaddle blankets, and I read three sleep training books in three nights.

(One morning after a particularly hard night, I overheard David in the kitchen, muttering to himself while making a pot of coffee, "So, what did you do last night? I stayed up all night. It's what I do every night.")

Finally, we found an answer. A friend swore by a new mechanical bed called a mamaRoo. I googled online reviews at 8 p.m. and triumphantly told Dave, "Honey, I think this one is legit." Even Amazon Prime two-day shipping was too slow for a sleepless parent. I located one in stock at our local Buy Buy Baby, which—thank heaven—was open until 9 p.m. I drove down the street and stopped at the red stop lights, looking at the drivers around me. They all looked so rested. I bet they slept all night, didn't have spit up on their clothes and got to take a hot shower whenever they wanted.

I bulldozered through the automatic glass doors of Buy Buy Baby, with bags under my eyes and greasy hair. I snagged a mamaRoo, swiped my credit card with glee and triumphantly lugged the gigantic box home like Santa with the perfect gift. Oh glorious, wonderful modern baby inventions! The mechanical bed hummed and Baby Esther was soon sleeping like, well, a baby. We gingerly transferred the wee babe to her pink princess bassinet and then dove under our sheets. (Just before my eyelids shut, my mind shouted, *It will be time to nurse again in three hours!* Sigh.)

Months passed and, finally, Baby Esther began to sleep through the night. (I think moms should get a free steak dinner when their child finally sleeps through the night.)

As Esther got older, one of the best parts of my day was getting her up from her nap. I'd open the door to her nursery and say, "Baby?" She was usually waiting for me lying on her stomach, a chubby hand holding the bumper pad down so her tiny eyes could search for me through the crib slats. As soon as she saw me, she would sit up, start flapping her little arms up and down like an excited bird and give me a big, gummy, open-mouth smile. Let me tell you, I felt like a million dollars with that greeting. I swept her up in an embrace, cheek to cheek. (There is nothing as soft as the flawless cheek of a baby, is there?) I let her feel my breath on the back of her neck for a few seconds and then planted a big, wet smooch on her button lips. Ah, those moments were my daily slice of heaven.

But mostly because she was sleeping through the night.

Stop and Smell: Isn't it fun being a parent of little children? Whether you have just returned from the grocery store or are picking them up from the church nursery, as soon as they spot you, they go absolutely crazy. It's like you're a famous celebrity or the president of the United States and they're your most loyal, ardent groupies. Their eyes light up, their little mouths drop open and they gasp in delight to see their beloved parent. I love kneeling down with my arms wide for a big hug from my little ones. Treasure these ecstatic hellos.

Stop and Reflect:

1. Which do you think are the easier to raise, girls or boys?

2. How does chronic sleep deprivation affect you?

3. How did you handle the sleeplessness of having a newborn?

4. If you are pregnant, how do you think you will handle sleepless newborn nights?

CHAPTER FIFTEEN

Life With Two Small Children

"I live in a madhouse ruled by a tiny army that I made myself."

–Anonymous

Life with a newborn and a two-year-old toddler for me was like waking up in a different world, drowning in a sea of floating dirty diapers. I wasn't prepared. I became a dazed madwoman playing—and losing—an eternal game of Whack-a-mole all day and all night. Change a diaper, wipe a toddler, slap together peanut butter sandwiches, feed the baby, clean up spilled milk, change another diaper, calm a toddler tantrum, change another diaper. Repeat cycle all day, every day. At first, I felt like an unpaid slave in a dirty uniform, working 24/7 while confined to simple, one-syllable little-people conversations. Adding another child doubled the love, but it also exponentially doubled the work.

I quickly figured out how to handle the transition from one to two children age two and under: never leave your house. I mean, how long does it take just to get in the car with two (or more) tiny dependents? An hour? It felt like running in mud. Nurse the baby, change a diaper, locate and slap on four tiny shoes, make Samson go the bathroom, strap Baby Esther into her infant car seat, lug the car seat to car and strap it in, toss in the diaper bag (wait, I forgot the wipes!), load the distracted toddler, buckle the toddler in … "Oh no. Is that a dirty diaper

I smell? Oh, dear. What do you mean you have to go potty, Samson? You just went."

When you arrive at your destination, it gets even crazier. Now you are still out of control but with a bunch of strangers gawking at you. How do you cross a busy parking lot spearheading a tiny caravan totally dependent on you?

I slung the diaper bag across my shoulder like a pack mule, lugged the baby in the infant car seat with one hand (good grief, that thing is heavy!) and gripped the dawdling toddler with my other hand. "No, Samson. You may *not* go the bathroom. We just got here. Okay, fine." The whole hoard of us would then squeeze into a tiny bathroom stall (please let the handicap one be open!). I'd change the baby's diaper while yanking Samson's shirt back to keep him from diving under the side to look at the lady in the next stall.

C'mon, guys. Where are the American entrepreneurs developing more drive-through options for parents of young children? I would pay through the roof to not have to wake a sleeping baby, then unbuckle my troop and drag them through dangerous parking lots. I celebrated the dry cleaner drive-through errand. It was a mom power trip. Boom—mission accomplished in 2.5 seconds with both kids. And the Starbucks drive-through mom caffeine fix? God bless you. I'm so sorry I vomited on you during morning sickness.

If I ever went out without the kids, I felt like the Energizer Bunny on steroids. I could knock out more errands in an hour than I could in a week with my two darlings. I was literally shaking with so much energy and adrenaline that I couldn't decide what to tackle first.

When we went out as a family, it was easier with Dave's help but still crazy. One day he turned to me like a general before battle. "I say we divide and conquer." He meant, *You take a kid and I'll take a kid and we'll start tackling the tasks.* How do parents handle three children? Zones?

Life with two small children spawned a mom who did things I had never done before. I shopped at Target with wet hair because I was that desperate to get both a shower and the shopping done while Dave was home. My hands deteriorated to man hands. I chopped off all my nails so they wouldn't snag the wee babe (who has time for nail polish?). My hair highlights grew out and, wow, did I need a haircut, but I just quit looking at the mirror. I almost exclusively wore nursing tanks and jogging suits and sometimes slept in them. I downed cold children's leftovers for most meals, when I remembered to eat.

On my worst days, I shoved the kids at Dave when he came home and yelled that I was leaving the house right then and there and going shopping. That usually meant I went to Target. I bought a coffee and "shopped" for nothing for an hour all by myself. I hope you never saw me there. I senselessly wandered the store with an empty basket sipping caffeine on my hour "off." When I returned home, I sometimes sat in my car in the driveway, doing nothing and enjoying the silence. After a few minutes sitting, I drew in a deep breath, and started to psyche myself up to return to Diaperland. "You can do this. You got this!"

I had never drunk coffee my entire life. But after my second child arrived, I religiously downed at least one Target-purchased can of Starbucks Doubleshot Espresso daily, post afternoon nap. Why? The time window between the afternoon nap and bedtime was the hardest. My friends called it the Long Hours. (Mamas, you KNOW what I am talking about.) The children woke up energized from their nap, but I was exhausted from plowing through multiple projects while uninterrupted and we still had dinner and bedtime to conquer.

(Since then, I've never skipped my afternoon coffee fix. One week I may or may not have bought ten four-pack cases of Starbucks Doubleshot Espresso. It also may or may not have been the only reason I went to Target.)

The nights were as wild as the days. Sometimes Esther would cry out, other times Samson would. On one particularly difficult night, Dave and I almost collided in the dark hallway between the kids' rooms. "Trade kids?" I asked. Dave sighed, "Sure." The next day we downed an entire pot of coffee in ten minutes flat.

A few weeks later, after another long night with teething Baby Esther, Samson bounced onto our king-size bed early the next morning. "Wanna play Batman, Mama?" Please tell me we're not the only parents in the world who have woken up on a Saturday morning, put a TV show on for their child and gone back to bed.

Some of my friends braved the grocery store with a newborn and a toddler. I would rather go skinny dipping in the Arctic Ocean. Samson and I once ate peanut butter and jelly sandwiches three times a day for three days in a row until I found time to go solo. When I finally made it to the grocery store, I slowly circled every aisle like a beady-eyed doomsday prepper, buying everything in sight. I needed our food supply to last a long time. Who knew when I could come back again? As I watched my items march down the belt toward the scanner, I felt like a modern-day Scarlett O'Hara shaking my fist in the wind with a hoopskirt fluttering behind me: "As God is my witness, we will not starve!"

I was checking out of the grocery store one afternoon, tired and haggard with bags under my eyes, with a full cart. The clueless checker made small talk while she scanned my hundred items. "Wow! You sure are buying a lot! Are you having a party? Or are you going camping?" she chirped, all bright eyed and well rested.

I thought of my two little ones and me at the house all day long day after day. "Kind of." I smiled. "Actually, yes. Camping and a party."

But, like a baby myself, I began to slowly change and grow in my new world. Instead of fretting over all the things I *didn't* get done each day, I started to focus on the things I *did* accomplish. I nursed Baby Esther five times. I cooked breakfast. I cleaned up after breakfast. I dressed both children. I bathed both children.

I realized that we new mothers *do* get things done. It just doesn't look that way at the end of the day. I also recognized that I needed to start letting things go. It simply wasn't the season for elaborate meals, an immaculate house and daily empty laundry hampers.

Stop and Smell: People kept telling me that "the working years" of parenting would be gone before I knew it. Sometimes I wanted to knock them flat on the ground with my floral diaper bag. It felt so permanent! I couldn't imagine a life without diapers. But they were right. As I write this, my life now is so different from how it was in this chapter—and it's only been a year. I now actually like going places with *both* my children!

I wish someone would've pulled me aside when I had Esther and reminded me that I will work hard for a short time but I will enjoy close-in-age siblings for life. Sibling relationships are often the longest lasting. Your children will most likely know their sibling(s) longer than their parents, and perhaps even longer than their spouse or their friends. My grandmother enjoyed her younger sister's friendship for over eighty years. Keep the big picture in sight. This season of drowning will soon turn into a natural stroke. You can do it!

Stop and Reflect:

1. What are some challenges you face in your current parenting season?

2. What are some solutions you have found?

3. What parenting advice has really helped you?

4. If you have two or more children, what sibling interaction do you love so far?

5. If you are pregnant, what is important to you as you parent the little years?

CHAPTER SIXTEEN

Slow Down

"Joy is found in simple things."

–Todd Stocker,
Dancing with God: First Year Thoughts on the Loss of My Daughter

Life with small children is *slow*. Just about everything we do takes much more time because each child needs help. After we brought Samson home, simple tasks like getting dressed, preparing to leave the house, getting in the car, eating (or should we call it feeding) and bedtime seemed to take forever. Then when our second child was born, the work doubled with consistent messes and interruptions. We moved at a snail's pace most days. If I tried to hurry, the mean mommy I hate emerged. (That's probably why I quit going anywhere at first!)

Life with small children is also *simple*, because we follow the same routine nearly every day: eating, playing, naps, clean-up, bath time, etc. Simple language, simple humor, simple tasks.

I am not naturally a slow-moving, simple-living person. I am a driven, energetic, type-A, high-activity, high-productivity, highly social girl. Small children felt like a train wreck at first. I couldn't get anything done. I resented the messes and interruptions, and no matter how hard I worked, I couldn't keep up. I felt like I was failing at this new life. I felt like a rented mule, beaten down each day with forced patience and flexibility. It seemed like all I did was put out fires all day long. I told myself this season of small children was not "me" and that I would be a better parent when my children were older.

But now, in these forced long, slow, simple days of caring for two small children, I am learning to change my perspective. Lazy days playing in the backyard, small routine tasks like eating the same breakfast over and over, simple joys like Samson discovering a roly-poly bug. I want to revel in the ordinary extraordinary slow, simple life of young children. I don't want to just get through or survive it. I want to smile and laugh and explore life with them.

I used to try to hammer out projects or clean up the house while the children were awake, but now I'm learning to pause and recreate myself as well. When else are we forced to slow down in life? Perhaps this season of motherhood is not a trial after all. Maybe it's a once-in-a-lifetime gift.

One way I'm learning to slow down is by thinking of the cycle of life. Someday I will be an old lady and Samson or Esther may be taking care of me. Instead of me holding Samson's little hand to keep him safe as we cross a parking lot, maybe my son will give me his arm to lean on as I slowly shuffle to a handicap parking spot. Instead of me hoisting Esther into a car seat, maybe she will open *my* car door, hold my grandma purse, and assist me as I slowly climb in. Instead of me buckling Samson in his car seat, perhaps he will buckle my seat belt because my hands are too shaky. Seeing a life perspective makes me care for my babies with a little bit more love.

Over the past two years, my parents cared for and buried two of their parents. I watched them do for their aging parents all the things I do for my small children: take them to doctor appointments, dress them, fix their hair and, yes, even spoon-feed them. I stopped to think, *I may be caring for my future caretakers.* This helps me gain fresh kindness as I go about my day tending my little darlings.

Another thing that helps me keep perspective is remembering something my father used to do. He often used a simple yet brilliant phrase to slow down his active brood of five children. He smiled at us all and said, "Here we are!" It meant that he wanted us to stop and savor the moment. He often used it when we were all together as a family doing something a little out of the ordinary. "Here we are ... eating breakfast by a lake." or "Here we are ... roasting marshmallows by the fire."

As a child, I never realized that he was conditioning us to become budding optimists. To see the glass half full. To be grateful for life's smallest blessings. That's the way I want to live, and that's the way I want my children to live.

In my quest to slow down and enjoy everyday life as a new parent, that little phrase, "Here we are!" took on new meaning for me when a friend was diagnosed with stage-four cancer. The news broke my heart, and I finally broke down crying in a Chili's parking lot late one night. I grilled Dave with my deepest questions about life and God's goodness in the midst of sorrow.

The next morning I awoke in cloud of grief, thinking of my friend. But during our normal scrambled eggs family breakfast, I remembered my dad's childhood phrase. I pierced the heavy silence with a timid ray of light: "Here we are!"

Dave looked at me, mid-bite, confused.

Filled with emotion at the stark contrast between terminal cancer and the beautiful young faces of my family, I stammered through tears, "It means, here we are! All together eating breakfast. Everyone is healthy and happy. We don't know what will happen in the future or even tomorrow. But we can always stop and appreciate the happiness of this moment."

Dave smiled, and ever since then we've tried to say the phrase, "Here we are!" whenever possible. At a restaurant after we've ordered our food. When driving in our car, as I look back at our two angels in their car seats. At night when I reach for Dave's hand in bed. We never know how short life may be. Enjoy the moment.

Stop and Smell: Unless you purposely stop in life to appreciate the here and now, you'll rush through each day often unhappy and unsatisfied. Instead of resenting the new-parent pace of life and simple tasks, be grateful for this temporary, once-in-a-lifetime magical slow season of young children. Try to find times in your day to stop and relish the moment with your small children. Say "Here we are!" when you sit down for a meal, pull out of the driveway in the car or when you take a walk. Savor today's special moments and anticipate tomorrow's rainbows. You'll only find them if you look for them.

Stop and Reflect:

1. How have you adjusted to your new slow, simple life with a young child—or young children?

2. How can you simplify your daily routine with your little one(s)?

3. If you are pregnant, do you have some ideas on how to make the transition easier when you add caring for a child to your daily routine?

CHAPTER SEVENTEEN

Let Go

"Happiness, not in another place but this place ... not for another hour, but this hour."

–Walt Whitman

Before children, I loved knocking out my daily projects. I blazed through the day with bulldozer-like efficiency and productivity. I made the Energizer Bunny weep with envy.

After my first child, I slowed down, but I could still do a lot. After our second child, however, the days and nights all snowballed into a blur. I worked as fast and hard as I possibly could and leveraged my efficiency by multi-tasking, calling stores to have items waiting, shopping online, creating systems, organizing, etc. But when I gauged my progress each night, I was shocked at how little it seemed I had accomplished. I could only sustain the basics of life.

I barely survived each day and hoped I could somehow get through tomorrow. I was stressed out and running ragged, snapping at my children and my dear husband. The days slipped between my fingers like sand in an hourglass. I wanted to slam on the brakes and enjoy my children, but I didn't know how.

Then I made a discovery. I couldn't stop my pace of life. But I could stop and enjoy my life, right smack dab in the middle of all the chaos. So I made two changes: I began to let things go around the house so I wasn't as stressed, and I started to intentionally stop and enjoy my little ones throughout the day.

Now I leave the folded clothes in the laundry basket overnight instead of putting them all away the same day. Sometimes I don't clean up the kitchen before I go to bed. We even eat cereal for dinner some days. If Samson asks me to read him a seventy-two-page picture book about Sammy the Seal, I try to stop what I'm doing and spend time with him. I want to view special moments with my children as one of the most important things I do each day, instead of thinking of all the other tasks I could be completing. I've learned that when my children ask me to read to them or play with them, if my answer is no more often than yes, they will stop asking. That thought makes me shudder. The work will always be there, but my children will not.

A wise mama treasures her family more than productivity.

Stop and Smell: What parts of life with small children do you enjoy? Maybe it's nursing or bottle time in the rocking chair, reading picture books aloud, sitting together at the end of the day to watch a show, sharing a snack mid-afternoon or taking your daily walk with your little one in a stroller. When you do these activities, stop and remind yourself of how happy you are. It's important to keep a positive outlook in the middle of chaotic days! You can do it!

Stop and Reflect:

1. When do you tend to get stressed most in your parenting adventure?

2. How do you avoid or successfully address those feelings?

3. Do you tend to prioritize people or projects more? How do you want to live?

4. If you are pregnant, do you think it will be hard or easy for you to adjust to a little bit more of a chaotic environment when your tiny one arrives?

CHAPTER EIGHTEEN

Double the Trouble, Double The Fun

"Looking into the eyes of a child is like looking into the eyes of Jesus."

–Bettie Hedgpath

Somewhere in the chaos of having two children age two and under, I realized that my happiness lay not in a getting a break or vacation, but in stopping in my everyday life to smell the roses. Extraordinary parenting moments were all around me. I just needed to change my parenting perspective to see them. Here are some of my ordinary-but-extraordinary parenting moments—maybe they will help you to discover your own!

* * *

Because Samson was obsessed with Baby Esther, he never left her side and I never left them alone together. So, when she was awake, the three of us traveled together in a little pack all around the house.

Once, while Samson was observing Baby Esther on her changing table while I was dressing her, he yelled, "Gross, Baby Esther! Gross!" He jumped off the ottoman that he pushed all around the nursery to observe the new baby's doings and trotted over to retrieve a burp cloth, all the while muttering the same words over and over: "Gross, Baby Esther! Gross!"

I was confused since she had not spit up. He jumped back up on the ottoman, gently swiped away the tiny bubbles she had been blowing at him and said, "Der ya go, baby." What a sweet big brother!

* * *

Dave fascinated Samson with some new black walkie-talkies. Ever since then, Samson attempted to talk to Baby Esther through her baby monitors throughout the house. (They are not two-way, but neither Dave nor I have the heart to break the news to him.) Whenever Samson heard her fussing, he darted to the nearest monitor and whispered into it loudly, "It all right, Baby Esther! It all right! Stop crying!" or "Baby Esther, don't worry! I come now! I come now!" Then he raced upstairs to drop a few of his favorite monster trucks into her crib to console her. How I love that little boy!

* * *

One of the sweetest sibling interactions I've seen was Baby Esther and Samson waving to one another at random times. I would be going about my day, washing the breakfast dishes, then suddenly I would spy Esther initiating a wave, silently with big eyes, and Samson responding. No words, just silent little waving sessions between two small people. They even did this at naptime, as if to say, "Good-bye for now." Baby Esther, on my hip, waving to Samson, cuddled in his bed, who was waving back. I stopped in wonder, watching them before carrying Esther to her room. Oh, time stand still.

* * *

To help forge good sibling relationships, we created nicknames for Baby Esther in honor of the funny things she did. It started the day I told Samboy that Baby Esther eats so many blueberries that she might possibly turn into one someday, so we must call her "The Big Giant Blueberry."

Samson laughed and laughed.

Then one day we discovered Esther downing cherries, seeds and all. Samson was mesmerized when I asked, "Baby Esther, how are those seeds feeling bouncing around in your stomach?" A funny nickname helped Samson to laugh and gain patience while I took care of his little sister. "Samboy, wait one second while I change the diaper for 'The Seed Eater.'"

Esther won another nickname thanks to her obsession with Samson's Crocs shoes. She loved wearing all our shoes, but Samson's crocs were the grand prize because they were easy for her to put on and keep on. We tried to hide them from her, but she sniffed them out like a hound. "Samson," I joked one evening, "go give 'The Croc Stealer' a kiss goodnight!" Wild laughing.

What do you do to foster positive sibling relationships between your children? How can you create a fun family atmosphere at your home?

* * *

Almost every summer morning, when the breakfast dishes were NOT done, I swept up Baby Esther, Samson and a blanket, and we all headed out the front door to … our front yard! I tossed our special blue blanket in the shade under a tree, then we spent an hour watching an occasional car drive down the street, choosing our favorite house and pointing out airplanes.

Samson enthusiastically waved at each passing car, but, his rate of a return wave was about one out of ten because the drivers seemed to be in a determined hurry and didn't notice our picnic party. (This makes me want to slow down and look around while driving!) Teething Baby Esther always tried to eat the grass and leaves, making Samson laugh his head off. Samson hunted ants and spiders to either watch or kill, depending on his mood. I told Samson stories while Baby Esther cooed and the wind rustled through the trees.

Try a front yard picnic with your little one(s) to start the day!

* * *

Sometimes when I'm out while Dave watches the kids, I get so excited about coming home to be with my little family. I wish I could get one of those "I'd rather be [insert hobby]" bumper stickers, but instead of "golfing" or "sailing," I'd put "at home with my family."

One day as I was driving home, chomping at the bit to see my little Samboy and the gummy smile of Baby Esther, I suddenly realized it won't always be like this. Someday, instead of diapers and spit-up, I'd have elementary-aged children, then teenagers, and then just Dave and me in a quiet home again. I can't wait for each special season in my children's lives, but I wish I could hit "pause" on life right now in our blissful world of pure and innocent darling little ones.

Have you thought of your future life as a parent? Enjoy your current season!

* * *

One day I fixed a simple breakfast for my little people. Esther was chomping a banana in her highchair on my left. (Aren't babies innately cute because they are just silent small humans watching everything you do with big eyes?) Samson was on my right, spilling and eating cereal.

Suddenly I felt something on my leg under the table. I looked under it to discover Samson had rested his foot on top of my knee. Immediately my mind reeled back to when he was a baby. Every time Samson would eat in his highchair, he would stick out a fat little baby foot, feeling around to see if he could find Dave or me. Once he felt one of our legs, he rested his foot on us, clamping our skin with curled baby toes. I think it made him feel more secure to be in contact with a parent. And there we were again, with my big four-year-old resting his tanned foot on my knee under our kitchen table. Never in a million years would I tell him to take it off.

In new situations, I notice my children often race back to me to lay a hand on my arm or hug my leg as they observe the New Thing. Don't you love that? You are their source of security, and they rely on you to navigate, whether something is scary or okay. The next time your child runs over to touch you for security, treasure that moment.

* * *

Samson turned into a fish last summer when we moved into a house with a pool. One night, I put Esther to bed and Samson and I hit the pool under the stars. He was enamored since it was 9 p.m., a whole hour past bedtime.

Boom! Samson plunged into the water, then churned his arms and legs like a speedboat coming toward me as I waited for him on the step. Right before he touched me, I swam to the other side. But when I grabbed the side, I popped my head up and gave him a big thumbs-up. "Samson! You are like a shark!" I told him. "That was fantastic swimming!" He shot both thumbs up back at me and was off again, following like a baby seal follows its mother.

Suddenly it hit me that this was a moment in parenting to relish. My baby boy and I were playing our very first swim game together. I couldn't help but think about what would've happened if I'd said no when he begged and begged me to get in the pool at the end of a long day. *No, it's past your bedtime ... No, Mama is too tired ... Okay, but you swim by yourself. I don't want to get my hair wet because I don't want to have to take a shower ... I just want to relax.* But I know the day will come when Samson won't incessantly ask me to swim with him, be with him, read to him and play with him. Until then, I will keep ruining my hair in the pool.

What was a fun moment you experienced with your child today?

* * *

One evening after dinner, Samson noticed raindrops pelting our backyard pool. "Look, Mama!" he cried. "It's raining!" I gasped, matching his excitement, "Let's go outside!" We bolted through the back door onto our covered porch. I sat cross-legged on our patio table, waiting to soak up the next ordinary, extraordinary parenting moments.

Brave Esther gasped in delight and streaked out into the pouring rain. Samson and I laughed and laughed. What was she doing? Soon her "water-fountain" pigtail of baby-fine hair on top of her head wilted. I stripped her down to her diaper and watched the raindrops slide down her smooth baby skin. Samson discovered a big yellow sun umbrella, twice his size, on the porch. He opened and closed it triumphantly all by himself, three times in a row, then dashed out into the rain, protected by the umbrella.

I remembered exploring the magical world of rain when I was a little girl. My wise mother released my four siblings and me into the front yard to dip our toes in the churning river chugging along the curb and to knead our bare toes in the soft mud. Now my baby boy and girl stood there in the rain, looking back at me.

Esther toddled up to me with eyes that looked bigger than usual thanks to the smashed wet hair hugging her fat cheeks. "Wah! Wah! Wah!" she told me.

"Okay, I'm watching, baby," I said. "Go!"

She staggered back to a big puddle, did a couple of

uncoordinated baby hops and then plopped down in a terrific splash of water. I applauded as if she'd performed in the best show on Broadway.

Samson was more cautious, stopping to listen to the rain drumming against the umbrella and tipping it back to feel the water pelt his toes. I started to tell him to not poke Esther in the eye with his enormous umbrella but refrained. *Why am I even saying that?* I thought. *Because boring adults have been saying it for decades? Not today.* I took their little hands in mine—Samson on the left and Esther on the right—and we ran together through the magical droplets.

One of the most exciting things about parenting my children is that I get the chance to help them form a positive life perspective—like enjoying, instead of bemoaning, the weather. Our children watch our reactions to life like a hawk. I'm sure you're doing a great job being a positive role model! Unless, of course, you have a sleepless newborn or a teething baby. Then you are totally off the hook.

Stop and Smell: Young children give us an incredible gift: the ability to enjoy the world through the eyes of innocence and curiosity. They are young only for a short time. The next time your little one says something cute or reacts in a childlike way, savor the moment.

Stop and Reflect:

1. What are some of the surprises of being a parent?

2. What experiences would you tell a new parent to be prepared for?

3. What advice would you have given yourself about parenthood?

4. If you are pregnant, what changes are you most excited about when your little one arrives?

CHAPTER NINETEEN

My Happy, Messy Home

"Before I had kids, I didn't even know it was possible

to destroy an entire house with a granola bar."

—@LurkAtHomeMom

Cleaning the house when you have young children is like shoveling rain. On days when I attempted to pick up the clutter, a tornado of toys and messes following right behind me. I didn't like living in the baby and toddler chaos day in and day out. It was hard to think clearly and positively when my house was in a constant state of disarray. My wise mother (who somehow always knows the parenting struggles I'm fighting) thoughtfully framed for me a poem that was her favorite mantra as a young mother:

The cleaning and scrubbing will wait till tomorrow, for children grow up, as I've learned to my sorrow. So quiet down, cobwebs. Dust go to sleep. I'm rocking my baby and babies don't keep.

I started to view the messes as beautiful, temporary flowers of a beautiful, temporary life with small children. One time when Samson "helped" me cook macaroni, he accidentally popped open the box and showered my kitchen floor with 594 uncooked macaroni shells. I yelled at him, but then asked for forgiveness. (I believe in asking your children for forgiveness when you mess up, even when they are young. It's good for them and good for you!)

Despite sweeping three times, I kept crunching shells beneath my feet while I was cooking. Instead of getting irritated, I tried to remind myself how delightful it was to have a little guy around while I was cooking. Wouldn't it be quiet and lonely without my little chatterbox chef?

Here are some of my favorite baby and toddler messes. Maybe these will help you view your little-people clutter differently.

* The little food and dirt smudges on the shoulder of my shirt at the end of the day. Aw, those are just paw prints from a baby holding a beloved mama while she carries the baby on her hip. They aren't dirt marks; they are love marks.

* Books scattered all over the couch and floor. It means I stopped my day to sit down with my two little darlings to share stories, laughter and fun. I think of my preschooler "reading" the books in his high-pitched voice and with jumbled grammar. I think of my baby holding a book over her head like the Statue of Liberty so I will read to her.

* Toys all over the backyard. I see the beautiful aftermath of long days full of imagination and slow child's play. Here's where Esther showed me seven different toys she discovered, all in a neat row. There's where Batman had it out with the Transformers in the sandbox for an hour.

* The pile of bathtub toys. I always smile when I swipe trucks, ducks and princess cups out of the bathtub. I think of Samson rolling his monster trucks around the rim of the tub and Esther sucking the wet washcloth. I think of gleaming little wet bodies and the fun hooded-towel aftermath, and how Samson and I always laugh at Esther proudly smashing lotion not on her body but on her hair.-

* My messy closet. I have a big closet, and my children love to play in it. At the end of the day, I stop to review with a happy sigh the six unmatched shoes Esther tried to wear, the three dresses on the floor from Samson hiding in the Hanging Clothes Cave and the littered socks from a sock war. What a boring closet I will have some day.

* Back porch mess. Our back porch is small and messy. Drying swimsuits and fun memories cover the chairs. The table holds our new special kinetic sand, a few plastic sand toys, a bug "jail" that Esther likes to hang around her neck, popsicle wrappers from a fun hot summer afternoon and a pile of shoes because we like to take our shoes off to "wee-lax," as Samson says. I wouldn't trade my Norman Rockwall porch with anyone.

* Car mess. I see Esther's favorite little "lovey" blanket and think of her holding it and sucking her thumb as she smiles at me in the rearview mirror. I spot four plastic boy toys and think of Samson's non-stop creative backseat play, with an occasional sacrifice of a toy to his whining sister. I love my car messes! (P.S. When I take my car to the car wash, I feel I should shove a fistful of five-dollar bills in the tip box. I shudder to think what they find. All I know is they return a clean car plus seventeen missing toys stacked neatly on the seat between the two car seats. God bless them.)

* Kitchen mess. My kitchen is almost always messy. Primary-colored sippy cups blanket the countertop. Random toys are scattered all over the floor and under the kitchen table. Spill stains and food fleck the floor, especially under the high chair. But when I stumble downstairs in the morning and view that never-clean kitchen floor, I make myself stop and savor the sight.

My children and I spend many happy hours together in the kitchen. They are my little cooking assistants. (Hurrah for the mess! It means I included them even though they made a mess and it took twice as long!) They are my little tasters. (That's why you have toys to pass the time between tastings!) And they are my fellow dining patrons. (Look at the three messy place mats and one high chair. How boring the table would be if it was clean and set for one!) I hung a small sign in my kitchen by the light switch so I would read it each day. It reads: "Good moms have laundry piles, sticky floors, dirty ovens and happy kids." Amen!

* Little smudges on windows and mirrors. There are smears on my bathroom mirror from a post-bath face-making party. And smudges on the glass back door from little hands begging to go outside to play. And—my favorite—smudges from baby hands and noses mashed against the front window, watching "Dada" drive off for work and waiting for him to return again. I almost don't want to clean them off.

Stop and Smell: When Samson was a toddler, my mother used to take him for us overnight so that Dave and I could have a date night and I could have a break. Each time I dropped him off, the first thing I did when we returned home was clean up the entire house because I knew it would stay clean for twenty-four hours until he returned. Ha! Living in Toyland chaos is hard, but if you try to remember to see beauty in the messes, you will grow less resentful and be happier. Soon you will teach them to pick up after themselves, but when you are outnumbered and they are too young, all you can do is change your perspective. You can do it!

Stop and Reflect:

1. What are your favorite baby or toddler messes?

2. Were you naturally an orderly or person before children? What about your spouse? Has that changed since you've become a parent?

3. What do you think is a good first clean-up chore for your child to learn?

4. If you are pregnant, how do you think you will react when your house grows messy with little-people clutter? How do you want to handle the new messes?

CHAPTER TWENTY

Eating With Little People

"Where's the cooking show with the baby hanging off your leg, screaming for a Popsicle, while you try to microwave a vegetable?"

—someecards[3]

EATING AT HOME WITH YOUNG CHILDREN

After Baby Esther was born, mealtimes overwhelmed me. Before children, I enjoyed cooking, but now I was too exhausted. It was difficult to care for two small children and simultaneously conquer menu planning, grocery shopping, cooking, feeding and clean-up. Meals felt like a balls from a never-ending fast-speed batting cage; they just kept coming at me, three times a day, 365 days a year. I sulked inwardly at food for a few weeks, thinking that if we didn't have to eat all the time, I would be a much nicer and less-stressed mother. (I mean, wouldn't just *one* meal a day be so much more doable? Ha!) I knew I needed to change my attitude and also my "cooking."

First, I worked on my meal outlook. If you think about it, mealtimes are actually a chance to stop and sit down together as a family and interact. Instead of viewing meals with dread and resentment, I tried to see them as a welcome interruption

---

[3] http://www.someecards.com/usercards/viewcard/MjAxMy1lN-WQ3ZTY5MzhmZWE5MThk

that provided quality family time and forced us to pause and enjoy one other. It's all about attitude.

Second, my meals got a lot simpler. For lunch, sometimes we eat a piece of deli meat, a slice of cheese and some grapes. We still dine mostly on Costco paper plates. I also keep three square vases stuffed with plastic knives, forks and spoons prominently displayed on our counter for ease of use and quick clean-up.

Even now, I still rarely eat a hot bite of anything because of the countless needs and interruptions. But I do try to enjoy the mealtime. We joke, laugh and talk about good things that have happened so far in the day. I catch up with my little people and my husband. A new attitude and approach has made all the difference.

A mama is the heart of the home. Let's set a warm mealtime atmosphere!

Here are some of our craziest (and most meaningful) mealtime stories:

* * *

When Samson was three, I slapped some reheated chicken spaghetti on his tray, a foolish meal choice for a preschooler. After he finished, I yanked a washcloth from the sink to wash him down, sighing at the looming kitchen clean-up. (First problem, the mounting clean-up stress ripe for unleashing on my innocent child. I hate it when I do that! I don't want to take out stress on them!)

Then I noticed Samson pulling noodles off his filthy shirt and throwing them on the floor. My eye bulged like an angry bull and I started to reprimand him. But I caught myself halfway through when I noticed the floor. Seemingly a thousand noodle casualties from a spaghetti-eating war covered the floor under Samson's chair. I burst out laughing at myself. How could I get angry at a few more noodles? (Second problem, it wasn't Samson's fault that I chose a naturally messy meal.) Samson looked up at me with a spaghetti sauce goatee, and suddenly we were both giggling with noodles all around us. Sometimes, you just gotta laugh in the small-child chaos.

Try to keep an internal parent stress barometer. If you start to get stressed about an external situation, remind yourself to keep that stress in check. Don't take it out on your innocent children. They naturally create non-stop interruptions and messes, and it's not their fault that they add to your stress. For example, when I cut it close on our time to leave the house and then Samson spills his milk, it's easy for me to let him have it because now we are going to be even later. But really, it was just a natural preschooler accident. I need to take a parent chill pill and remember the bigger picture: nothing is worth yelling at my children, and I need to plan better next time.

* * *

EATING OUT WITH YOUNG CHILDREN

Before children, Dave and I turned up our noses at fellow patrons who stuck a portable movie in front of their children at a restaurant. "Look at that," I whispered to Dave. "They're killing their child's brain cells." I'd then flip back my perfect blonde hair that I had 1.5 hours to fix before dinner.

Fast forward to when we had a two-year-old and a baby of our own. *If* we decided it was worth it to attempt a restaurant with both of them, Samson toted his own iPad in a monogrammed case and pulled out black earphones the size of Kansas. It was like a date night with our children present. If we forgot the iPad, we pulled up YouTube videos of his favorite shows on a cell phone. (Look at all these golden insider tips you are getting for free.) If anyone looked at us funny, I just turned my greasy blonde bun that I'd slapped up in 2.5 seconds the other way.

The first thing we do when we sit down at our table is slide all the utensils and cups away from the grabbing baby. (Parents, am I right or am I right? We all do the Baby Table Swipe as soon as we are seated). Before the server can even greet us, I bark, "Hi, can we please get some waters. Do you have a kids cup—with a *lid*, or else he will spill. Can you bring that right away? They are both *really* thirsty. Oh, and we are ready to order *now*. Yes, that will be it. Can you please rush our order? Just bring the check with the food."

While we wait, Esther downs six saltine cracker packages and a sugar packet while I'm not looking. After we eat, the floor looks more like dogs ate there than people did. We try to clean up as best we can, slap down a gigantic tip and dash out fifteen minutes after arriving.

* * *

One time, two-year-old Samboy passed a gumball machine as we entered a restaurant. (Why in the world do evil people jam those temptation machines in the worst possible location—the area when you enter or leave places? Can't we parents all toss the evil people a bunch of quarters to burn those things?) Anyway, Samson started crying for a gumball, and of course, toddlers cannot have gum. We had driven a long distance to try this new restaurant, so we were not leaving. We waited in line for a table for twenty minutes and finally sat down to order, but the gumball crying escalated.

Even after two bathroom training visits, Samson was still dragon toddler (Samboy, you know I love you, but I have to tell the story like it really happened so other parents know they are not alone). Finally, mad-as-a-hornet-and-hungry Dave scooped up the bawling boy and declared, "We're outta here."

I'm pretty sure the patrons applauded when we walked out the door. I call it the Parent Walk of Shame. Our child won, we lost. My advice for new parents: if at first you don't succeed, get the heck out of there.

I have learned, no matter how much training and planning you do, you can't win 'em all. When little-people situations escalate and your perfect preparation craters, just shrug your shoulders. "Oh, well. Maybe next time." All parents of young children experience stress. It's up to us how we respond. Laugh or cry, smile or pout. You can do it!

* * *

Once we stopped in for Wednesday night fajitas at a local Mexican restaurant. Samson kept whining that his stomach hurt. We ordered him a Sprite and looked over the menu. Five minutes later, he vomited a Sprite-and-food tidal wave all over himself, the table and Dave. Without a word, Dave scooped up bawling Samson, both of them drenched in vomit, and we walked right out the door.

Have you ever had to walk out of a restaurant because of your young child? Can you laugh about it now?

* * *

One day we took both kids to the local waterpark. Afterward, we decided to try and brave Chipotle for lunch. The kids were tired, cranky and hungry, so we took nothing by chance.

We slowly drove into the parking lot like Navy Seal snipers, sniffing out the number of cars to detect the number of patrons. (Too crowded? Not worth it.). It looked promising so Dave grabbed Esther and the diaper bag, and I dragged whining Samson across the parking lot with the Handcuff Grip (Toddler parents, you KNOW you have used the Handcuff Grip).

We ordered like madmen. While Dave paid, I snagged the diaper bag and Esther, then hauled a wooden high chair to a table. Not just any table—the one closest to the drink refills, the condiments and the bathroom. (You don't mess around when you have young children.)

By the time the steaming food arrived, Esther had scarfed down half of her diaper bag snacks and two lollypops, so she was not even hungry anymore and was crying to get down. Like a ninja on steroids, Dave cut up all the food into tiny pieces with a black plastic fork and knife. (Dave's child-size-bite cutting skills would make Jackie Chan weep with envy.)

But as soon as sunburned Samson took a bite, he yelped, "It's too hot! I'm hungry!"

We blew on their hot food until we were red in the face, fake laughing to get Samson to quit crying and join in on the so-fun food-cooling game. I shoveled some of my food to Esther, most of which she swept to the ground, including a mound of sticky rice, because she was full from downing an entire container of banana puffs.

I didn't make eye contact with our appalled fellow patrons who, considering their perfect figures, perfect clothes and perfect clean tables, didn't have young children. Samson finally tried the cooled chicken but immediately started bawling again. "It's yucky! I don't liiike it!" (Apparently, someone—who will never be my friend—had over spiced today's chicken.)

I marched past all the people waiting in line and shouldered my way to the manager, because parents of screaming children cannot wait. (A crying child promotes you to VIP—very important parent.)

"Hi," I barked, smoothing my slightly wet hair back and trying to gain authoritative composure, but subconsciously knowing I looked like a demanding drowned rat in a damp swimsuit cover-up. "My son can't eat his lunch because the chicken is way too spicy. Can you please just make him some plain cheese enchiladas?"

Finally, both children were eating something for a few minutes, so that was when Dave and I downed our meals in 2.5 seconds. I looked up at Dave mid-bite and said, "My love, when is eating out ever going to be relaxing again?"

Remember this wild season of young children is short-lived. At night, after the children go to bed, Dave and I often relax in bed and reflect on our day. We remind each other of funny or sweet things our little ones did or said. This helps us to stop and revel in the little years instead of resenting them or being overwhelmed. Tonight, maybe you can think of some memories from your day with your child.

* * *

We rarely eat out sans kids, but when we do, we arrive at 5 p.m. with the senior citizens because we're used to eating early with kids. Out of habit, we ninja-chop our expensive steaks into tiny pieces and finish our entire meal so quickly it's embarrassing. (It's hard to break the new-parent mantra: eat when you can as fast as you can.)

"Done already?" chirps the well-rested young server.

I wish we had a cool response to that question by now. But instead, we fake laugh sheepishly, "Heh, heh. Yeah, we have small kids, so we're used to eating fast." God bless parents, one and all.

Stop and Smell: One night, when our family was eating dinner at a barbecue buffet restaurant (we do live in Texas, y'all), I suddenly noticed the family at the table next to us. There sat a calm father and mother, slowly eating their hot food, uninterrupted, along with two blonde sons about six and eight years old. I elbowed Dave and whispered like it was a celebrity citing, "Look at them! Maybe that's us in a few years!" We drooled a little and returned to our cold food. The little years are a temporary season. Laugh and enjoy it!

Stop and Reflect:

1. Are cooking and mealtimes stressful for you? What has helped?

2. Do you have any fun memories of eating out with young children?

3. If you are pregnant, how do you feel about eating out with young children? How are you planning to balance cooking and caring for a baby?

CHAPTER TWENTY-ONE

Traveling With Young Children

"You know you are a parent when going shopping at Target by yourself feels like a vacation, and going on a family vacation feels like work."

—someecards[4]

Yes, I was the young mom on American Airlines flight 3442, row ten, whose nine-month-old had vomited all over himself, his mother and the floor after landing in Baton Rouge. It was a long fifteen-minute taxi ride in and everyone smelled the rank vomit. There was nothing I could do. Everyone had to stay seated. It was even more fun surrounded by a dozen LSU frat boys in starched shirts who had been drinking beer all during the flight. Talk about feeling like an uncool new mom.

When we arrived, I Olympic-walked through the airport covered in vomit, holding a baby covered in vomit, and shoved him into waiting Dave's starched plaid shirt. "Let's get out of here," I muttered.

Has your darling ever vomited in public? It's a red-letter day in Parentland. Welcome to the club!

---

4   http://www.someecards.com/usercards/viewcard/MjAxMy04O-TE4NzRjMmJmYzA0YWUz

Samson was a year old when we made the worst traveling-with-kids decision of our lives. We decided to take him on a cruise to Bermuda. It included a three-hour flight to Baltimore, a long ship ride over the Atlantic Ocean to Bermuda and a two-time-zone difference that destroyed his sleep habits. The turbulent ship, coupled with his unsteady new walking legs, caused him to vomit constantly from seasickness. There were no kid-friendly areas on the boat. He skipped naps and cried all night long, waking our neighbors on the other side of the paper-thin walls.

After a full week of no sleep, he was totally off schedule and over-tired for the long flight home—and so were Dave and I. We crammed into our economy plane seats with businessmen nestled all around us. Perfect. Let the fireworks begin for the Wall Street fat-cat neighbors.

Samson lost it one hour into the flight, screaming inconsolably. We tried everything—snacks, movies, suckers. Finally, we tried to give him a bottle since that always worked. Dave jabbed it in his mouth. Silence. Beautiful, lovely, coveted silence. Suddenly, as if in a horror film sequence, Samson slowly pulled back from the nipple and screamed even louder.

I grabbed the baby and the bottle and marched down the tiny aisle, smacking a few elbows and legs on our way to the bathroom. *What in the world could be wrong with him?* I asked myself. I soon discovered the problem. Apparently, I had forgotten to remove the white plastic wafer that prevents the bottle from spilling before usage. Starving Samson hadn't been able to get any milk.

After landing, we almost vowed to never, ever travel again with children. (New-parent takeaway: if it ain't broke, don't leave the house.)

But we did. Two years later, we agreed to travel to from Texas to California—with a six-month-old and a three-year-old—for a family vacation. When we sat down in our seats for the three-and-a-half-hour flight, I turned to give Esther her bottle so she would fall asleep for the duration of the flight, full and happy. I suddenly realized in horror that I had forgotten her bottle. Her *bottle*! We had a starving baby and no way to feed her (I had just finished nursing). Dave stared at me in disbelief. "Really, honey? The bottle? You forgot the bottle?"

(New-parent takeaway: When traveling with young kids, less is never more. Bring everything.)

We somehow survived the flight, but when we arrived, we encountered a new problem. Dave yanked all of our checked items off the black luggage belt, then we looked around in dismay. We had a baby, a preschooler, three suitcases, the diaper bag, the carry-on bag full of Samson's toys, a stroller, two car seats and a Pack 'n Play. How in the world could we get everyone and everything to the rental car booth? Where is Mary Poppins when you need her? We looked like the Beverly Hillbillies of Dallas.

* * *

Last September, we stayed at a Dallas hotel for five days during Dave's annual work conference. We decided to take the kids with us and soon realized it was a great choice. As the poor valet guys unloaded the fifty absolutely essential baby and preschooler items, Samboy asked question after question in that annoying squeaky toddler tone that I've grown to love. But he suddenly stopped mid-sentence at the sight of a revolving door, mesmerized. He had never seen one before. (I try to never belittle new experiences like revolving doors or downplay or make it "normal." I want it to be as exciting as my child believes it is!)

I demonstrated to Samson how it worked, then invited him to give it a try. For as long as I live, I will never forget my little white-haired boy in his pastel blue polo shirt pushing that door around and around. He was bent in half with his head down, both hands pushing with all his might. *Ka-POW, Ka-POW, ka-POW*, the door sang merrily. Finally, scared that he would get sick from so many circles, I yelled to my tiny bull, "Awesome! Now jump out, Samboy!" With one final shove, he popped out like a piece of toast from a toaster, and spun around to gawk in awe as the doors continued to spin.

Dave's company graciously upgraded us to a huge suite. When we entered (after stopping to demonstrate the "magic" room key card), Samson and Esther ran around and around in circles in our new "home," laughing their heads off. Dave and I each hoisted up a little body so they could smash their noses against the gigantic windows to view the city skyline. Samson yelled with glee, "Look at da big baw!" (Dallas's Reunion Tower resembles an elevated ball.)

At our first hotel restaurant breakfast, I led Samson over to the buffet for a waffle. His eyes grew as wide as saucers at seeing all the food and he chose one of almost everything. Dave and I laughed, watching him take one bite out of twenty different items. Back in our room, Dave and I prepared to leave for a business lunch. I gave instructions to the babysitter, then turned to Samson. "Samboy, you can order something for lunch when we leave." Without hesitation, he replied, "Okay, I would like mac 'n cheese, pizza, a hamburger and milk."

Every time Samson mashed the magical elevator button, Dave, Samson and I dashed to one of the six potential elevator doors to see who would "win" the right door that would open first. And every time we turned down the hotel hallway to our corner room, Samson and I raced—even when I was wearing heels—to see who would get to our door first.

When we finally left the hotel to go home, Samson bawled and begged us to go back to our "new home." Our trip was ten times sweeter because we had our two little darlings.

Stop and Smell: If you're brave enough to travel with young children, you have to get in the right frame of mind before you slide into the car or get on the plane. You can google "child travel tips" until you're blue in the face, but you can't control everything that happens. Decide to laugh—or at least stay calm—when things get hairy. As hard as traveling with young children can be, Dave and I have shared many of our best parenting moments while on trips. (But between you and me, I still think it's an unfair deal when Dave takes the older preschooler who watches a movie the whole flight while I struggle with the toddler who wants to get off my lap non-stop. All Dave has to do is push "play." Hmmmm. Maybe I will secretly sneak Samson a Red Bull before our next flight. Bwahahaha. Mom's revenge.)

Stop and Reflect:

1. What's your favorite traveling-with-young-children story so far in your parenthood adventure? (And if you haven't tried leaving the house yet, that's okay, too.) Did you laugh or cry?

2. Do you think traveling by car or by plane is easier with a young child?

3. Where would you like to travel with your child someday?

4. If you are pregnant, how do you feel about traveling with a baby?

CHAPTER TWENTY-TWO

Married With Children

"A worthy woman who can find? For her price is far above rubies."

–Proverbs 31:10, ASV

It's hard to enjoy your children when your marriage is on the rocks.

The transition from married couple to married-with-two-small-children couple wasn't easy for Dave and me. After Baby Esther arrived, I felt completely overwhelmed and our marriage suffered. (Someone once told me that when you have a child, your husband gets half a wife.) It wasn't because we didn't care about each other. We were simply chronically exhausted and stressed out from caring for the constant needs of a baby and two-year-old night and day, with little time or energy left for our marriage.

That's when we decided that we had to make some changes. We needed marriage maintenance in the diaper-blizzard years. Sure, we could hope our marriage would somehow survive and hope to reconnect when the kids were older. But who wants to live like that? We didn't want to emerge years later as haggard strangers. We didn't want a child-centered home. Our first priority was our marriage and then our children. We strongly believe that one of the greatest gifts we can give our children is a mom and dad who love each other.

One Thursday night, Dave and I booked a babysitter and sat down at Starbucks—with Doubleshot Espressos thanks to teething-baby sleepless nights—to jot down some ideas on building our marriage while parenting small children.

Here are some of those ideas that seem to help Dave and I stay connected during this chaotic season. (Each marriage is different, so these ideas may or may not be helpful for your family and situation.) It is possible to enjoy a great marriage in the wake of babies; you just have to work at it. You can do it!

1. **Extend grace when you are dog-tired.** Whether it's because of a newborn, teething baby, scared toddler, or sick child, sleepless nights are a bear. You naturally snap at your children and spouse when walking around like a zombie during the day. Every small annoyance seems like a huge deal when you're in a cloud of exhaustion. Purpose in your heart to overlook offenses and extend grace to your spouse. You're just not yourselves.

2. **Connect once a day with your love.** Dave and I felt disconnected soon after Baby Esther arrived. We felt more like co-workers at the same daycare, instead of husband and wife. Now, after the kids go to bed, we try to take ten minutes to debrief about the day and just talk. We sometimes individually retreat after the kids are in bed and then make an effort to connect as a couple before lights out. Some of our other friends talk right after the kids go down and then relax individually. Discover what works for your unique family dynamics!

3. **Just say "No!" to busyness. Eliminate potential conflict.** Now is not the time to over-commit the calendar. We learned this the hard way. Dave and I experienced so much conflict early on because we were, bottom line, too busy. Mondays followed over-committed weekends that left us disconnected and exhausted—a prime recipe for blow-up "discussions." After a few heated battles post over-scheduling, I returned to

my role as social dictator with renewed resolve to just say no. It's not worth the fights or overstressing the kids. Our little family comes first.

Each Sunday after church, when the kids go down for their naps, Dave and I meet for a scheduling meeting. We lug our calendars to the kitchen table and go over the coming week. If it looks too busy, I cancel events, reminding myself of the terrible fights post over-scheduling. This is not the season to say yes to everything. It is the season to say no to most and yes to a few. You may offend some people at first, but protecting the sanity of your family is more important.

4. Weeknights and weekends. Talk through expectations for weekday nights and weekends when both parents are at home. Remember what's happening. When dad returns from work, he is tired. At that same time of day, mom is exhausted, too. Both crave a break, but there are those adorable little ones still needing attention, dinner and bedtime. And what about the weekends? Perhaps the mom envisions a family time, but dad may want to knock out projects or go play golf.

Discuss expectations and formulate a good mutual plan of action. You'll both have a better attitude about weekends and weeknights if you know what to expect and try to honor each other's needs. Too many fights stem from poor communication. Parenting is new territory, so keep talking!

5. Recreate yourselves individually. In the wake of parenthood, both spouses can feel like they eat, sleep and breathe small children. (And we really do breathe them, if you count smelling diapers. Ha!) A mom and dad who never take a break are miserable. Make a list of what recreates you as an individual. Maybe it's a hobby, working out, social time, shopping or a sport. Then build daily or weekly schedules so you can both recreate yourselves individually. It feels selfish at first, but this, alone, has eliminated so much tension because

we're not running on empty. We leave tired and return refreshed, recharged and a better parent and spouse.

6. Support your spouse. Dave and I decided we would try to "be there" to support one another for big moments. For example, I cheered Dave on when he ran a biathlon, and Dave was in the front row, filming with his iPhone, when I sang a song in front of a big audience. Because we experienced these moments with each other, we feel connected and supported. It doesn't always happen, especially when you have to arrange babysitting or have a nursing baby, but when possible we do our best to support one another at significant life events.

7. Make fun memories. I remember rocking Baby Samson and overhearing Dave talking on the phone to one of his high school guy friends. They were laughing and joking about old times. We naturally associate fun with certain people because our connection to them is through fun activities. Unfortunately, our spouse can easily morph into just a roommate and fellow caretaker during the small-children stage, if we're not careful.

Try to create fun memory-making experiences to laugh and talk about later on. Soon after Esther was born, Dave and I joined our church softball team. We couldn't make every practice or game, but when we did, I remember the fun we had together in the crisp autumn air. Plus, we had great memories to talk about on the drive home and throughout the week. I know it feels like you have no time or energy to even *think* about arranging childcare or researching a new activity, but I promise you it's worth it. Our marriage is as interesting and fun as we make it.

8. Shared growth experiences. We try to learn new things and grow as a couple, whether it is through a structured class or reading a book together. Sometimes we get involved in a parenting class, a church small group, a new hobby or a mission trip. We also commit to one marriage conference a year.

During those experiences, we are both learning and changing as individuals and as a couple. We have new material to discuss as a couple. Before we implemented growth activities, we felt that our date night dinners had deteriorated to mere check-ups on each other's individual lives. Grow together!

9. Marriage maintenance get-away trip. If you have grandparents or a babysitter you trust, try slipping away for a weekend with your spouse. The first time we planned a trip, I was so worried about leaving the kids that Dave told me to cancel our flight because my anxiety would ruin the trip. That was a wake-up call for me. I promised I would change my attitude. If I could give my children almost every day and night, I could give my husband and my marriage a long weekend.

That trip was better than our honeymoon! We laughed, talked and had a blast making fun memories together. Plus, we enjoyed a full night's sleep, hot meals and uninterrupted showers. We left with a stronger marriage and a solid resolve to take at least one trip sans kids per year. Try it if you can. You and your marriage will be so glad you did!

10. Date in the middle of the diaper blizzard. Ever since we married, Dave and I have tried to go out for a date once a week. But when our second child arrived, it was so difficult to schedule dates with nursing, naps, bedtimes and arranging childcare. We went months without one. The solution? We now schedule permanent childcare on a certain night of the week. We are much more likely to follow through since the childcare is already set up.

When we go on a date night, Dave and I both try to pull ourselves out of our parenting and work identities. We take time to dress up for each other. It sure makes me fall in love with Dave all over again when I see him getting dressed in something special for "our time," and I try hard to dress like his girlfriend instead of a tired mom in stained workout clothes. (Uh, yes, I totally run errands in workout clothes.)

I'm not going to lie. Often, we don't talk for the first thirty minutes as we slowly unwind from high energy and stress, but then we start to relax, eat and talk. Each week, as a tired mother, I look forward to our date night more than anything else.

* * *

We did not implement all of these changes the day our second baby was born, nor do we do all of them simultaneously. We've just found that *proactive* ideas like these have helped. We are no longer tagging marriage-building activities in when we remember to or feel like it. We try on a daily and weekly basis to build our marriage. Sometimes our efforts fall through because of a sick child or over-scheduling, but when we're able to maintain them as a whole, our marriage is strong and so is our parenting.

I also know that some couples may disagree with so much emphasis on marriage over children. Some mothers wouldn't dream of leaving their babies or having their children "sacrifice" for the marriage. But for our family, we really want our marriage to be first. Our family began when Dave and I married, not when we added children. We love our kids, but we love our spouse more, and we want our lifestyle to reflect that. Give your children the best gift and foundation to start their life: parents who have a strong marriage!

Stop and Smell: Great marriages don't just happen. They take work and investment, especially when a marriage competes with the responsibilities of young children. Being a mom or dad is not your only identity. You're also a spouse. It's easy to get tunnel vision in the little years, thinking only about your children because they need so much care each day. But don't neglect your marriage or the love of your life. You can do it! Besides, what else would you talk about during date night if you didn't have those adorable munchkins?

Stop and Reflect:

1. Do you put your spouse before your child or children? Why or why not?

2. What recreates you individually?

3. How has having young children affected your marriage?

4. What seems to help support your marriage while parenting young children?

5. If you are pregnant, how are you planning to keep your marriage strong after the baby arrives?

CHAPTER TWENTY-THREE

Slow Down and Enjoy Your Children

"We must return optimism to our parenting. To focus on the joys, not the hassles; the love, not the disappointments; the common sense, not the complexities."

–Fred G. Gosman

When you bring a new baby home, your life suddenly becomes a lot busier than before. And if you have more children, it becomes exponentially busier with each one.

It was hard for me to find ways to slow down to enjoy my children in the middle of chaotic, non-stop days—especially when we brought home our second child. But through trial and error, I discovered some simple ways to revel in my little ones, instead of bulldozing through each day. Here are some ways that help me to s-l-o-w down ... maybe they will help you, too.

1. *A morning song.* Each morning when I open my children's curtains to let in the sun, I try to sing a cheery song to start the day. Mothers are the heart of the home, and what better way to set the tone for the day than a merry heart and tune! My mother sang to me each morning, and now I greet the day with my little ones with a happy song. Sometimes I need it more than they do after a sleepless night!

2. *Wake up slowly.* My favorite part of the day is the morning, because I get to greet my two tiny angels. Instead of viewing the morning routine as a necessary evil, I try to enjoy it. I purposely allot plenty of time to lollygag, smile and talk about the Samson's latest dream. We take our time getting dressed, and I try to kiss their little foreheads at least three times before breakfast.

3. *Happy mealtimes.* Mealtimes, no matter how simple the menu, can be an excellent time to enjoy your children—three times a day! We always start with a prayer and then I try to make an effort to discuss one happy topic, whether it is a story about my children obeying or the best part of our day. If you are in the silent baby stage, look at your child's dirty face and big eyes and remember how fortunate you are to share meals with your little blessing.

4. *Cheers!* Sometimes when my children and I are enjoying a drink together, we stop and toast the occasion. For example, in the morning, I raise my coffee mug to Samson's sippy cup, smile and say, "Cheers!" He taps my cup with his and pipes in return, "Cheers!"

5. *Relax after meals.* "Relax" is a word I try to use after mealtimes to cultivate a loving, comforting home life. After we finish our (often chaotic) meal, I smile and say, "Hey, guys, I have a great idea. Let's go *relax* in the living room!" We then melt into the couch cushions after the children grab their favorite blankets. Sometimes they play with toys and sometimes they ask me to read them a book. But most of the time we just silently relax.

6. *Read a picture book aloud.* I try to read at least one picture book a day to my children. They love the affection they get by snuggling in my lap or by my side on the couch, and I try to revel in their sweet smell and rapt attention.

7. *Go outside.* Sometimes, when caring for young children all day, you can feel isolated in your own house. Nature offers renewal for tired parents, entertainment for the restless toddlers and preschoolers, and calms fussy babies.

8. *Car seat kiss.* Strapping children into car seats can become routine and bothersome, so I try to make it a special moment. After the last click of their restraints, I kiss their little cheeks. It helps me pause and appreciate my two little angels in the middle of mundane errands.

Stop and Smell: Try to carve out time in your week to build fun memories with your child. Stopping to enjoy my children is still not easy for me. Oftentimes I would rather clean up a dirty kitchen than read a Curious George picture book aloud. If you are like me, take heart! It just takes time and willpower. One thing that helps me to keep perspective is to ask myself, *In twenty years, how will I feel about how I spent this day?* Make smaller decisions in your parenting day based on your big-picture parenting goals.

Stop and Reflect:

1. Have you found ways to slow down and enjoy life with your children?

2. What do you enjoy doing with your child the most?

3. What prevents you from enjoying your children? How can you avoid that?

4. Do you have any ideas for a fun date with your child?

5. If you are pregnant, what activity are you looking forward to sharing with your child? It could be something you already enjoy or just something you've always wanted to do with your own child.

CHAPTER TWENTY-FOUR

Stop And Enjoy Your Children

"Children will not remember you for the material things you provided but for the feeling that you cherished them."

–Richard L. Evans

Sometimes it can feel like you are just putting out fires all day long while caring for little ones. Here are some ways to transform daily tasks into special moments by stopping to enjoy your little one in the middle of your task!

1. STOP when changing diapers. Once when I was changing Esther's diaper, I looked down at her face. She was studying me and my movements with fascinated attention. I felt so bad. How many diaper changes had I rushed through without any eye contact or interaction? Now I try to make diaper changes a special moment between my child and me. I myself stop and revel in her cuteness. Sometimes we practice animal sounds or new words, and sometimes we play silly games. Now diaper changing is one of my favorite tasks instead of just another duty.

2. STOP when taking out or collecting the mail. When Esther helps me, she grabs the letters to deliver with the seriousness of a little soldier on a special mission. I hold her tiny hand as she steps off our front porch to the pebble walkway down to our black metal mailbox. She usually drops at least

one envelope in the dirt and smashes another one in half, but I keep telling myself that this moment is far more important than crinkled letters. I hoist up my chubby angel, and it takes her on average several pushes to discover the correct way to get the mail to slide into the mailbox. Then comes her favorite part: slamming the door shut with all her might. If she helps collect the mail, I give her a piece of junk mail that she proudly delivers to "Dada."

When Samson helps me, he likes to (surprise, surprise) do it all by himself while I watch from the doorway. He proudly saunters down the walkway, looking back over his shoulder every now and then to ensure I'm still watching his independent big-boy activity. He yanks open the mailbox door after a few tries (it sticks), then jams all the letters in while I bite my lip, knowing he is mashing half of them. He smacks the lid shut and gives me a thumbs-up with both hands.

If he collects the mail, he usually drops half of it on ground but immediately says, "Uh, dat was an accident, Mom." No problem, buddy. I hope we deliver and collect wrinkled, dirty mail for a long time.

3. STOP when driving. For most of my life, I looked at driving as a means to an end. I am an over-achieving, first-born German girl. Naturally, I've always wanted to leverage otherwise-unproductive driving time. I returned phone calls, checked e-mails at stoplights and stacked errands so close together that I had no time to even think about turning on music.

When Esther was a few months old, I arranged for Dave to keep her while I whisked Samson out the door for a pool playdate with friends. I put Samson into his car seat and buckled him up like a rodeo professional tying a cow's legs together. *Boom*—done! I jumped in my seat, slammed on black sunglasses and reversed my car down the driveway like I was breaking out of jail.

My mind reeled from all the planning and preparation for this little outing with Samson. The baby was fed, diapered and scheduled. I mentally checked off my list of sunscreen, swimsuit, towel and sack lunch for Samson. As I snatched my phone to return long-overdue voicemails, a small voice came from behind me: "Mama! 'Member dat place, Mama? 'Member dat?"

I glanced back at my little boy, who was pointing out the window at the new frozen yogurt shop where he'd enjoyed a dad-approved gigantic sprinkle-covered yogurt sundae the week before. "Yes, I remember that place, buddy." But I wouldn't have if I'd been on the phone. I slowly set my phone down and turned my ears on.

For the rest of the drive, Samson and I talked about each location he recognized. I told him a story about a dinosaur that ate rainbow-colored candy clouds. I drove close to a school bus so he could wave at the children. By the time we arrived at the playdate, I'd decided that I would change the way I drove with children in the car. Driving doesn't have to be simply a means to an end or an empty space to fill. Car rides can be magical parenting moments too, if we stop to enjoy them. Talk, tell stories and rock out to some of your favorite tunes.

4. STOP and have a party. The summer that Samson turned four, we moved to a house with a pool. I was determined to teach him how to be a kind host who welcomed his guests with love and warmth (even as a selfish toddler—ha!). So, before our first pool party, I told him about his friends swimming in our pool and how much fun we all would have. "It's going to be awesome, honey!" I said. "Everyone will come swim in our pool. It will be like a party!"

Halfway through our ordinary swim playdate, Samson ran to me dripping wet. He looked up at me through his hilarious bright green frog goggles and gasped, "Mama! This is a great party!" In the hot Texas sun, I laughed down at the tiny wet man and shouted with outstretched arms, "Yes, it is! It is a great party, son!"

From then on, Samson started seeing usual events as parties, and as a result, so did I. My favorite is when Samson says it at our house, during our normal mealtime at our normal kitchen table, "Mama! The whole family is here ... We having a family party!" I respond, "Yes, we are! A family party!" And if you think about it, anytime you are with your family for an everyday meal, it really is one of the best parties in the whole world. I cannot think of any other party I would rather attend.

5. STOP and hold your children. Someone once told me to always say yes if my children asked me to hold them because I'll never know when they will ask for the last time. One night, when Samson was almost four, he asked me to hold him on our way to bed, reminding me how big he is now. I picked him up, awkwardly cradling his big body. His long legs kept hitting doorframes as we passed through. I slowly laid him down on his bed and then stroked his soft white post-bath hair while I sang to him the same simple song, "Be Still and Know that I Am God," that my mother sang to me when I was a little girl. I prayed over him and for his future wife. I kissed his forehead and whispered the same thing I say every night, "Love you with all my heart."

Stop to hold your babies. It's a short-lived privilege.

Stop and Smell: Parenting young children can eat your energy and day faster than greased lightning if you don't watch it. Try to proactively carve out time in your day and week to build fun memories with your child. My dad used to rotate taking one of his five children each Sunday to the local doughnut shop to nab doughnuts "hot off the line" and share a fun, one-on-one breakfast. It's like going on a date with your spouse—you stop just living together and start building a good relationship. Date your child!

Stop and Reflect:

1. Have you discovered any daily tasks during that you can purposely enjoy the moment with your children?

2. How can you stop today to make a moment with your little darling?

3. If you are pregnant, do you think it will be challenging for you to stop to enjoy your child in the middle of a busy day? Why or why not?

CHAPTER TWENTY-FIVE

Potty Training Is For The Birds

"Well, Mommy, I don't want to disappoint you,
but I'm just sitting here until you give me a gummy bear."

—HaHasforHooHas.com

They say you know you're potty training when you have a potty in the kitchen and candy in the bathroom. I say, yeah right. It's more like thirteen empty juice boxes in the kitchen and a mommy crying in the urine-covered bathroom.

Oh, potty training, you are a delightful beast.

When we potty-trained Samboy, a friend recommended an e-book titled *Three-Day Potty Training—Start Friday, Done Sunday!* Subtitle: "The Queen of Potty Training will share tips, advice, and secrets to potty training in only three days." With a catchy title like that, how hard could it be?

Like a naïve new mother who had never potty-trained before, I read the book and decided to do it just as the book described. You go, girl. I went to Walmart and bought thirty pairs of little-boy underwear and a Lightning McQueen potty for twenty-two-month-old Samson.

The author reiterated over and over that this was to be a positive interaction and that negative words or tones of voice from a frustrated parent would quash progress. I was to put the underwear on my toddler and shadow him all day long while routinely chanting in a Pollyanna singsong voice, "Let Mommy know if you have to go pee, okay?" I practiced that phrase a few times privately in my bathroom in front of the mirror to ensure my intonation was upbeat and peppy. I sounded like an overzealous potty-training Who from Whoville. If Samson started to go in his underwear, I was to sweep him up and take him to the toilet, let him finish, change the underwear and do it all over again. All. Day. Long.

Samson was successfully potty trained by the end of three days, but I have never in my life felt so pushed in patience. Pulling nasty wet underwear off over and over? Wiping up urine all over the house? Keeping a calm tone when it's happened twelve times in a row? I felt like the clean-up girl for a never-ending urine parade.

* * *

Dave is a much more patient parent than me. (I will refer to him for the rest of this story as Patient Dave). He's level headed and it takes a lot for a child to frustrate him. For some incredibly unfortunate reason, Patient Dave always catches me at my worst as an impatient mom. (Like when it's taking twenty minutes instead of two minutes to get Samson dressed in the morning because he has the energy of twelve Red Bulls by 9 a.m. I finally yell, "Samson! Why aren't you paying attention? This would be over in two seconds if you would just concentrate!" I follow with a mature eyeball roll and a loud groan. At that very moment, Patient Dave pops his head in the room. "Seriously, honey? And we're trying to teach Samson to be in control of his emotions?")

Back to potty training. One night I was up late into the night with fussy Esther. So when I heard Samson crying at 2 a.m., I turned over in bed and kicked sleeping Patient Dave in the leg. "Honey, can you please check on Samson? He's crying and I am *so* tired."

Samson had surprisingly wet his bed. I overheard Patient Dave forcing the crying toddler to change pajamas and then telling him he could sleep in our bed. Samson was being a bear (sorry, son, but you were), crying about not liking his new pajamas and making many other toddler complaints and demands. (I was fake sleeping the whole time so I wouldn't have to deal with it.) Finally, the three of us were quiet in our king-size bed in the dark. Then Samson whined again, this time for a "Kweenex" for his runny nose. I heard Patient Dave sigh, get out of bed again and mutter, "What else do you want? A steak dinner?"

I burst out laughing from my fake sleeping. Finally! Patient Dave had snapped! (Insert wicked and inappropriate cackling by fake sleeper.)

Unfortunately, I still have to potty train Esther next year. I don't normally delegate my mom duties (I mean, this whole book is about reveling in them), but if I did, it would be potty training.

Stop and Smell: I wish I could give out shiny gold stars to new parents as they complete parenting stages. Nursing, done! Teething, done! Potty training, done! First ear infection, done! Sleeping through the night, done! Maybe you and your spouse can find a festive way to toast your parenting accomplishments. (I'd suggest dinner out, but you may have lost your appetite with all the potty talk.) Cheers to you!

Stop and Reflect:

1. Are you a naturally patient parent? How about your spouse? How do you try to keep an even tone and demeanor when parenting emotional little people?

2. What was your experience with potty training like? Did you keep your temper or lose it?

3. What was something funny that happened during potty training?

4. If you have *not* potty trained before, how do you feel about it? Are you going to be more proactive, or be more laid back in your approach? Do you think it will be easy or hard?

CHAPTER TWENTY-SIX

Getting White-Hair Perspective

"Never underestimate the power of perspective. It can change everything."

–Anonymous

One way I've learned to gain perspective as a parent is by interacting with older generations. This certainly includes grandparents, but also any other elderly friends who come into my life.

Dave and I occasionally take our children to visit with a dear older gentleman who I've known for half my life. He taught me how to play golf when I was a teenager, and now we visit him periodically in his assisted living home. He always wears a collared shirt with a bronze American flag pin and clip-on suspenders, and his stark white hair is always combed meticulously.

Throughout our dinner in the large dining room with red velvet curtains, he proudly introduces us to all his white-haired friends. Then we ride the elevator to the second floor to visit in his small apartment. He lost his wife many years ago but still keeps his table set with her pretty china as if they are just about to share dinner again. Two and half hours later, we load our tired little ones into the car. Although he is in his eighties and uses a gold-tipped cane to shuffle along, he insists on going with us to the parking lot and closing my car door like he always has—the perfect gentleman.

While we bring our children hoping to brighten his day, when we pull out of that driveway, life lessons knock the wind out of me. His generation is so over the typical pace of life in modern-day America: tearing through our days, teeming with productivity and focusing on quantity instead of quality; ensuring our kids have every opportunity to be successful, educated, and cultured; keeping up with the Joneses instead of the weather; using social media instead of forming real relationships; slapping activities on our calendar instead of joking around for half an hour. His generation recognizes the important things in life—family, relationships, faith, love. Help me, Lord, to see the important things each day as a parent.

I wish I could spend an hour each day with these wise, aged saints. Each wrinkled face brims with love and refined character forged from decades of lessons. I know many live with debilitating illnesses, but they still smile in the face of adversity. I hope I can reflect their life perspective—positivity over circumstance—each day as I tend my young family.

These residents are truly polite with perfect manners, never in a hurry to end a conversation. They patiently ask the names and ages of our children, comment about each child and tell me about their loved ones. They remind me that my baby girl is beautiful and excuse my restless toddler with graciousness. Can I be patient with toddler conversations and shower that same type of kindness to my children each day?

One afternoon, I took Samson to visit this same gentleman because he'd had a fall and now couldn't walk. Samson chose a G.I. Joe cup as a vase for the fresh flowers we were taking with us. On the drive over, I explained to him how we were going to cheer him up and show him love, and how our friend was a little sad because he was sick and that we would make him happy with the flowers and by giving him a hug. I was thrilled because I felt this was the first time Samson understood what "ministry" was about.

When we arrived, I smiled as my little man in his Batman T-shirt rattled off the ABCs, incorrectly spelled his name and recited a Scripture and the Pledge of Allegiance for our patient friend. When Samson finished, the gentleman offered him a Lifesaver mint as a prize. They were more than eighty years apart in age, but they both had white hair and needed each other. Samson cheered him up, but he was also teaching Samson—and his mother—life lessons.

When we stood to leave the magical, slow world to return to our fast-paced life, our friend stopped me. He told me with a glimmer in his eye that, although he was getting old and his body was not bouncing back the way it used to, he could still control his attitude and focus on the positive.

I smiled and nodded, but thought, *Wow. You can't walk, you've been sick for months, your wife passed years ago, you live all alone and you can barely eat. What stellar character!*

How can I complain about how hard motherhood is when I hear his response to much more difficult circumstances?

Before we left, our friend thoughtfully transferred the flowers to another vase and handed the G.I. Joe cup back to Samson. "Here, young man," he said. "I bet you would enjoy this a lot more than I would." I made Samson say thank you, but inside I made a note to slow down to show more kindness like this.

Stop and Smell: Try making friends with some admired parents who have older or grown children. Meet with them (or call them if it's too hard to leave your house—ha!) to tell them of your struggles and listen to their anecdotes. I love my fellow new-parent friends who are in my same life season, but

I've learned how important seasoned-parent point of views are, as well. Let them encourage you with their "big picture" life perspective during these diaper-blizzard years!

Stop and Reflect:

1. What helps you gain perspective as a parent?

2. What can you do today to reflect on the most important things in life?

3. If you are pregnant, what can you do after the baby arrives to keep perspective in your new, busy life with a baby?

CHAPTER TWENTY-SEVEN

Newbie Parent Stories

"You are making it difficult for me to be the parent I always imagined I would be."

—someecards[5]

As a new parent, sometimes it's easy to think that everyone else has parenting so much more under control. Not true! Life with little children inherently invites craziness, no matter who you are. Here are some of my new-parent stories. You are not alone.

* * *

Locked Car Woes

My car is equipped to automatically unlock all four doors from the driver seat. This handy mom feature allows me to easily get Samson out of his car seat, which sits in the backseat behind my driver's seat. But for several weeks, after I hit the "unlock" button, his door would still be locked. I would then hit the button again and again until it finally unlocked. Dave and I got so frustrated with this problem, especially while standing in steamy Texas summer parking lots, that Dave took it to the dealership to get it fixed.

---

5   http://www.someecards.com/usercards/viewcard/MjAxMi1iM-2RiNzJiYmRkNTY5YjBi

The mechanic told him that they ran all sorts of tests but found nothing wrong. Imagine our disbelief when we again encountered the same problem when we took our car home. Irate Dave took the car back to the dealership, with Samson in his car seat.

As Dave again explained and demonstrated the trouble to the mechanic, he suddenly discovered the problem. Every time the door unlocked automatically, Samson saw the shiny silver door lock move by his feet and kicked it back to lock it again. He thought it was a fun game. It was only when we rapidly hit unlock and then yanked open his door before he could kick the lock that we could open it. Dave profusely apologized to the raised-eyebrowed young mechanic and drove off, laughing.

Can you remember a crazy situation you have found yourself in with your child?

* * *

Crab Fears

You know how they say parents shouldn't model fear in front of their children so their children won't develop those fears? One morning, I took Samson out in the ocean for a swim. Just as we passed the point where the waves were breaking, a horrible crab snapped my toe. Instead of giving a mature, calm parent response, I screamed and started jumping like I was on a hot bed of coals. "Ah! Ah! A crab just bit me, Samson! Run! Run!"

I handcuff-gripped Samson's little wrist and dragged him through the waves toward shore as fast as I could, causing him to start bawling. I finally scooped him up (because who knew if there were other blood-hungry crabs about to attack) and limp-sprinted the final yards as fast as I could with a bleeding toe.

We plopped down on the sand side by side, my adrenaline and blood pumping. I burst out laughing at myself and then turned to try to calm sobbing Samson. I was panting, but breathlessly tried to convince him that my toe didn't hurt, that crabs only live in very deep water and that ocean swimming is so fun. He paused, took another look at my bloody toe and screamed even louder. I guess I'll model a brave parent another time.

Have you ever been a "bad parent" example? Can you laugh about it now?

* * *

Late-Night Creative Parenting

Sometimes parenting toddlers requires you to think outside of the box. One night, Samson was overtired from swimming all day when Dave innocently noted, "Yeah, your eyes look a little red from all that swimming."

Samson lost it. He started crying in terror, wailing, "But I don't want red eyes! I want blue eyes!" The more we tried to calm him, the louder he cried. It was almost 10 p.m. and everyone was exhausted.

Suddenly Dave placed his big hand over Samson's eyes so Samson couldn't see. Then he stammered through laughs, "Oh, Samson! I forgot! Sometimes if you blow on the eyes, the red goes away. I will try it ... Close your eyes!"

I clapped my hand over my mouth to stifle giggles while Samson kneeled dutifully with his eyes closed. Dave blew for a few seconds on each eye. Samson opened his eyes and Dave yelled, "It worked! Look, Mom, his eyes are blue again."

I echoed him, "Oh, yes! Wow! It worked. Your eyes are blue again."

Samson smiled in relief and got in bed. Crisis averted and bedtime saved.

How have you creatively parented? I don't know about you, but I still don't know what I'm doing many times! When things get really dicey in public, I turn to the gawking strangers and announce, "If it looks like I don't know what I'm doing, it's because I don't know what I'm doing."

* * *

Chuck E. Cheese Lesson

When Samboy was three, he played air hockey with a six-year-old boy at Chuck E. Cheese. Samson invited him to play and put a token in to begin the game. Samson's speech and playing ability was much more primitive than his opponent's due to the age gap, but Samson didn't care. He was having blast, laughing and smiling the whole time.

Then halfway through the game, the older boy slammed the plastic puck right into Samson's goal. He threw back his head, laughing at my sweet little boy with a pointed finger, "LOSER!"

Never in my life had I felt such a tidal wave of emotion come over me. I didn't say anything because Samson didn't understand that the other boy was making fun of him. Samson just smiled in return, innocently responding, "You did it!"

I wanted to bite that boy's head off and sweep my little angel back to a home that showered him with love and kindness. Right then and there I knew my mama-bear instincts would need to be bridled for the future. My children will be treated unkindly in life. And I remember a wise mother once reminding me that sometimes the toughest lessons are also the best growing experiences for our children's faith and character.

But that day at Chuck E. Cheese, I wasn't in the mood to build Samson's character. I wanted to trounce that little boy at air hockey and laugh back at him. (What had happened to me? Get your mama emotions under control, Leah!) It reminded me of Elizabeth Stone's poignant quote: "Making the decision to have a child—it is momentous. It is to decide forever to have your heart go walking around outside your body."

Have you experienced the mama-bear reaction when another child hit or made fun of your child? How did you respond? How do you want to respond in the future?

* * *

Sunday School Humility

At eighteen months old, Esther loved her little Sunday school class at church. One morning, we got in the long check-in line with the other parents and children. Finally, it was our turn and we approached the smiling nursery worker. While we answered the check-in questions, I picked Esther up to hold her on my hip. To my horror, I felt a tiny, completely naked rear end on my arm under her beautiful pink Sunday dress. Apparently, she had no diaper on when we left our house, on the drive to church and all the time up to that moment—and she was NOT potty-trained!

I turned to Dave with wide eyes in front of the nursery worker. "Honey! She has no diaper on!"

There was nothing to do but get down on my knees right there in front of everyone and awkwardly finagle a diaper on her, using her dress as a modesty drape. Oh, parenting. You humble me faster than anything I've ever experienced in life!

Have you ever forgotten something important when you went out? Can you laugh about it now?

* * *

Waterpark Fears

Unfortunately, Samson once had a bad experience at the wave pool at our local water park. He was a brave preschooler and begged to ride in a circle tube in the deep end. Sure enough, a gigantic wave flipped him over, leaving him shaken. When we visited the wave pool for the first time after the accident, he stood in ankle-deep water with his back to the deep end as the waves began. I sat on a tube a few feet from him in my pink mom baseball hat and matching swimsuit, watching him face his fears through cheap black sunglasses.

After a while, he turned around and smiled at the waves. Then he began punching and hitting the waves as hard as he could. Each time they rose at him, he smashed them with both hands, yelling triumphantly, "*Hi-YAH, hi-YAH!*" You could tell he was scared when the wave rose, but he used that adrenaline to conquer his fear.

As I watched him, I made myself promise to remember, in these next few years, that I am mothering a little man-to-be. I want to always encourage him in his strength and confidence so he can be brave as an adult, a silent superhero for his future family and world. Thank you, wave pool, for helping Samson conquer fear—and for the long nap afterward!

Has your child ever been fearful of something? How did you help them face their fears?

* * *

Silence is not always golden with young children. One time toddler Esther had been quiet for some time, so when I finally heard her squealing and laughing from the bathroom—a big no-no room for her—Samson and I dashed in to investigate. There she was happily slapping the toilet paper in one long piece into the toilet, over and over. Samson thought he would help by flushing the toilet. That sucked down the roll even faster, madly spinning it to both children's sheer delight. They squealed and laughed while I pushed them out if the way to slam my hand on top of the now-almost-empty roll of toilet paper to prevent a clogged toilet. Then they both started crying and I started laughing.

Have you experienced any funny toilet paper or bathroom antics with your little darling?

* * *

Dictator Mom

Toddlers and preschoolers often want to do everything by themselves. From getting dressed, to buckling their car seat, to making decisions about what they want to eat and drink, they want to be in control regardless of screaming babies, tired mamas, timetables, etc. I realize it's a natural and appropriate transition as they learn to do things themselves and start gaining independence, but when life turns into a child-dictated world, I hammer down on the decisions Samson and Esther can make. They make little to no decisions until they can obey me with no whining.

Apparently, I have been a bit too heavy-handed of late. One morning Esther was destroying Samson's bedroom while I tried to get Samson ready for the day. I was totally burned out with his preschooler independence. By golly, *I* was going to make all the decisions and he was just going to obey if it was the last thing I did. After *I* brushed his teeth, *I* yanked a T-shirt *I* chose off a hanger and barked, "Next, take your pajamas off and get your underwear on. *You* may choose your underwear."

Samson lit up like a Christmas tree. "Wow! Okay! Thanks, Mom! All right!"

Gee whiz, what had happened to me? Lighten up, Mama!

*Have you ever found yourself going overboard in your parenting?
Can you laugh about it afterward?*

* * *

Reading Out Loud

I'm not a big craft mom or a big baking mom, but I am a big reading mom. We cart home enough library books to fill Noah's ark. Samson and I tear through them in a few days, and I cannot tell you how wonderful it is to watch my boy taste humor, subtle plots, fantasy and character development with my old beloved picture book authors. I constantly study his eyes and face with my peripheral vision as I read aloud, ensuring my pace is right and my intonation is entertaining. Most importantly, I watch his reading comprehension like a hawk. If he seems to drift, we stop and recap. Most of the time, he gets it though. It is just magical when a tiny-toothed smile breaks in perfect harmony with a punch line.

At home, usually after breakfast, I pull a stack of books out to read. Samboy burrows into me and sits still as a stone—unbelievable since he is so energetic—for as long as my voice holds out. At naptime, I lie down next to him in his car bed and read easy chapter books like *Frog and Toad*. One of the most precious parts of reading together is that if I ever laugh at the story, he laughs too, even if he doesn't get what's funny. These are the best ways to spend an afternoon, lying in a car bed, side by side with my preschooler, sharing a laugh together.

One of my favorite events during reading time is when Samson needs to temporarily leave to nab a drink or his blanket. He pops up in the middle of a book, furiously yelling over and over, "Don't read until I get back, okay, Mom? Don't read ANYFING!" He keeps yelling and looking back over his shoulder while running away toward the bathroom or kitchen to check that I am not reading.

When we take long road trips, I turn our car into a library bookmobile. I gather board books for Esther and picture books for Samson. I let them each look at one book at a time, and when they're finished they trade it out for another one in the bag. I often hear Esther making sounds for the animals she is studying and Samson "reading" his books in his own words.

Unfortunately, we did encounter a rare reading problem. Dave and I, being the awesome type-A parents that we are, bought Samson the book Curious George Goes to the Aquarium in preparation for our big visit to the Texas State Aquarium in Corpus Christi. When we reached the sea-creature-touching area, Dave lifted Samson up to touch the animals. Samson immediately reeled back, yelling, "No! No! The crab snapped George's finger!" No matter how many times we assured him these animals wouldn't bite him, Samson recoiled in terror. Thanks a lot, Curious George.

Is reading aloud to your children challenging or fun for you? Does your child enjoy it? There is so much research to back the benefits of reading to little people. You can do it! P.S. It's okay to think about other things while reading. I do!

* * *

Batman

I always told myself I would never spoil my children by buying them tons of needless toys, producing ungrateful, entitled, sulky teenagers. No, my children would only get toys on special occasions and grow up grateful. Then came Batman. (Frozen Moms, you *know* what I am talking about.)

One crisp spring morning, a house on our street advertised a garage sale. Since I rarely went anywhere with two small children, I took them on a little walk in the stroller to view the leftovers. Samson spied a blue vintage Batmobile toy and three action figures: Robin, the Joker and Batman. I bought them for a dollar.

That night, Dave found a Batman show on Netflix, and that was the beginning of Batman mania. Samson was obsessed unlike he'd been with any other toy in the past. (Good-bye, Thomas the Train and Lightening McQueen.) We bought him a Batman night light, toothbrush, clothes, swimsuit, hooded towel with pointy black ears, every Batman book that has ever been written, etc. Every time I saw a Batman item in a store, I imagined Samson's response if I brought it home. I couldn't stop.

The week before Christmas, I stopped by Toys 'R' Us to buy ONE Batman present for Samson. I don't know if it was the sappy Christmas music playing or the bustle of all the frenzied parents, but I exited through the automatic doors like Batmom with a cart overflowing with Batman toys. I bought so many that I literally couldn't get my car's back door to shut. I sheepishly looked around the parking lot to see if any jokers were looking (no pun intended), then shoved the door shut with my superhero strength. On December 25, our house would become Gotham City and I couldn't wait.

The next summer, I bought Dave a Batman costume with fake muscles for Samson's Batman 4th birthday party. We blasted the Batman theme song through a bullhorn as Batman Dave burst into the party. (Just between you and me, he performed some amazing somersaults for a thirty-something dad.) Apparently, the guests were a little young for Batman. Half of them started crying, and no one wanted a photo with Batman except Samson.

After the party, I noticed Samson was in dire need of a new haircut. He told me he would like a Batman haircut. I smiled and said, "What does that mean, sweetie? Like short?" He responded, "No, Mom. It means I have two pointy ears."

So, if you see a child walking around with two horns of white hair, he's mine.

Has your child gravitated toward a certain toy? Have you ever gone overboard buying your child something? Do you or your spouse tend to buy more for your child?

* * *

Wet Wipe Wars

Boys will be boys, no matter their age. One day Dave started a wet-wipe war with Samson. They wadded wet wipes into snowballs and pelted each other across the living room. (For the record, they went through 482 wipes, friends. 482.) Esther gleefully scooped up the leftovers to toss in the air, laughing her head off. I didn't know what was happening until I came downstairs to discover wipe-snow blanketing the entire living room. Samson sheepishly threw a wipe toward me, leery of mom's response to the gigantic mess.

"What?" I yelled, mock-serious. "What did you just do?"

And it was Wipe WWII.

Do you have to clean up every mess your children make, or can you sometimes laugh and join in the fun? I love the look of surprise on their face when I burst out laughing instead of yelling.

Stop and Smell: One important thing to remember as a new parent is that you are constantly learning, growing and changing as a parent, right alongside your growing and changing child. Be gentle with yourself. This is all new territory. You are a baby parent, so don't beat yourself up over mistakes along the way. All parents, no matter how perfect they look, make mistakes. I do! Some days I wish I could have "do-overs," especially when I have yelled at my little angels. We just have to keep moving forward and laugh and learn from our mistakes! You are doing a great job!

Stop and Reflect:

1. What's a funny new parent story that has happened to you?

2. When have you been most embarrassed as a new parent?

3. If you are pregnant, how do you think you will handle embarrassing parenting moments in public?

CHAPTER TWENTY-EIGHT

You Know You're A Parent Of Small Children When ...

"Don't worry, you are not the first mom who's ever thrown a towel over the peed-on sheets and gone back to bed."

—Hallmark "The Edge of Motherhood" card

Parents of young children are like a secret, special sorority. We go about our day in a very different way from most of the world. How are we different? My friends and I brainstormed the list below. Enjoy!

You know you're a parent of small children when ...

*All your Netflix recommendations are children's animated movies.

*You know what a "lovey" is. (A small, soft blanket with an animal head that little children become obsessed with. If you lose it, they cry their eyes out and will not nap or sleep at night. Thoughtful parents purchase two and trade them out so they will wear out slowly.)

*You go out to eat as a family at 5 or 5:30 p.m. at the latest so the restaurant will be empty except for senior citizens and you stay thirty minutes max.

* You have not slept through the night for two years.

* Your children wake at 5 or 6 a.m. and sometimes you put them to bed at 6 p.m.

* Getting ready to leave the house takes at least twenty minutes of preparation.

* You sometimes have cereal as a meal twice in one day.

* You can never spontaneously ask another couple to "ride with us" to an event because your car is dominated by car seats.

* You ask for a child's cup with a lid every time you eat out. Every. Single. Time.

* You turn into dragon lady every time a delivery man ignores your "Please knock" sign and rings the doorbell right in the middle of naptime.

* You know what a fruit pouch is. (One of the best toddler and baby snacks ever invented.)

* Your kitchen is constantly littered with bottles and primary-colored sippy cups.

* You are willing to spend hundreds of dollars on sleep props—blackout-curtains, sound machines, etc.

* Your average lunch is leftover mac 'n cheese, frozen chicken nuggets or hotdogs.

* You find yourself still watching Disney Jr. thirty minutes after the kids are in bed.

* You can sing every word to [insert favorite cartoon theme song] and you sing it in the shower.

* You and your husband finally have some time without

the kids, and you are still saying things like, "I need to use the potty."

* You reheat your coffee a minimum three times before you actually finish a cup.

* You choose errand destinations based on drive-thru availability. No distance is too great for drive-thru services with young children.

* You can't take a shower without hearing phantom crying.

* You think sleep sacks and swaddle blankets are the best inventions of the century.

* You know every fast-food, take-out and delivery restaurant in your area like the back of your hand and have them on speed dial.

* You watch your baby monitor more than actual TV.

* You've wiped your child's runny nose with your bare hand.

* Your child wipes their nose on your clothes.

* You've used paper products at dinnertime for so long that you can't even remember what color your "real" plates are.

* You can change the baby's diaper blindfolded in five seconds while simultaneously lecturing your toddler.

* You can ninja-chop a child's plate of food into small pieces in 2.5 seconds.

* When you eat out sans kids, you still ninja-chop your own food and often finish your entire meal in five minutes, forgetting that you don't have to rush.

* You never leave the house without a diaper bag, an extra change of clothes for the children, snacks, a sippy cup, a bottle and Desitin.

* You actually write "take a shower" as part of your daily to-do list because you are that busy.

* You have ever tried to keep your tired child awake in the car so they would take a good nap at home. (A lost nap is a double negative. The child is cranky the rest of the day, and the parent never gets a break. Skipping naps is just not an option in our world.)

You know what I mean. You check the rearview mirror and notice your little one is about to doze off, with the child's head, like a big pinball, slowly bouncing from side to side in the car seat. NO! You ask your sleepy one ten questions in a row, very loudly. Then you repeatedly open and close the child's car window, all the while blaring loud music. If that doesn't work, you turn the music volume up and down, repeatedly. You dance and yell like a madman, watching the child like a hawk in the rearview mirror. If they start to doze off again, you get twice as crazy. Repeat until you pull in your driveway. When they take their long nap in their own bed instead of taking a car catnap, you sigh in happiness. It was totally worth it.

I've done it. And I don't care who saw me.

Stop and Smell: Life with small children can be one crazy circus, but learning to laugh at the chaos conquers the dicey situations. Develop friendships with other new parents so you can laugh off the stress together with fellow comrades! Tell your crazy stories and listen to theirs. Text a photo of your chaotic house or child covered in flour to a friend or your spouse. Laughter is good for the soul.

Stop and Reflect:

1. Which one of the examples above do you relate to most?

2. Which examples would you add to this list?

3. If you are pregnant, do any of these sound strange to you? Do you see any that might happen to you as a new parent?

CHAPTER TWENTY-NINE

Night Swimming

"Be happy in the moment, that's enough. Each moment is all we need, not more."

—Mother Teresa

One busy summer day, our schedule got kicked out the door. In the afternoon, I plopped both tired, cranky children into their little beds and let them nap until 5:30 p.m. Dave was gone overnight, but I was determined this wouldn't be just a survive-until-dad-gets-home kind of night.

I had no magical plans, but I started to scheme ways we could enjoy the rest of the day. Since they had a late nap, I decided allow the kids to stay up late. "Samboy!" I smiled down at him in the quiet kitchen. "Want to go outside with Mama?"

My little man charged out the back door with his toy pop gun, his tired mama lugging his sister in tow. We meandered down toward the swing set in the dusk. The fading rays highlighted our brown backyard grass, scorched by the merciless summer sun.

"The moon! Mama! Look at da moon!" Samson kept talking about the moon, and I finally realized it was because he rarely saw it since his bedtime was early. "Oh! The sand, Mama! Let's play in the sand!" he begged next.

I looked down at his squeaky-clean body and shampooed hair, fresh from his nightly bath. I then surveyed the damp wooden sandbox full of dirty toys. "Yes! Yes! Yes!" I agreed.

Samson and I played monster trucks until the blue sand stuck to every crevice on our skin. (Our sandbox has blue sand. It's hard to find, but what kid wouldn't prefer *blue* sand? I love to watch his little friends' eyes light up when they see it.) Then I threw another curveball: "Wanna go swimming under the stars?"

Splash! Samson hopped in our pool, fast as a hiccup. It was quiet and dark, and we both reveled in the quiet night without any words. I sat on the side holding Esther, my legs swirling in the water. Soon I would need to break the magical night and tuck the chlorine-soaked boy and his sister into bed.

I read Samson his nightly Bible story, this time about Queen Esther, but that night I skipped all the text and just created interesting dialogue using the pictures. We prayed and Samson had me pray for every friend he had ever met in his short years of life. Then I kissed his soft cheek and said, "I love you with all my heart!" Samson responded, "I do!"

On my way to bed, I spied the destroyed playroom, the piles of dirty clothes and the kitchen screaming my name. It would all be there tomorrow. I was so glad I chose to swim under the stars instead.

Stop and Smell: Pause during your day to do at least one non-mom task with your child. It can be as simple as eating a snack on the back porch, reading a book under a homemade tent or hunting acorns around your neighborhood. Break routine with fun. You will enjoy your children more and create fun memories to carry you through the challenging times.

Stop and Reflect:

1. What is your favorite thing to do with your child these days?

2. Do you feel torn between parenting moments and keeping up the house? I do!

3. How do you navigate your day to accomplish your priorities—both your practical tasks and bigger priorities like enjoying your children?

4. If you are pregnant, what are some ways plan to stop to enjoy your new baby, even when you are tired and overwhelmed?

CHAPTER THIRTY

A Walk On The Beach

"What it's like to be a parent: It's one of the hardest things you'll ever do, but in exchange it teaches you the meaning of unconditional love."

–Nicholas Sparks, *The Wedding*

When Esther was eighteen months old, I took her for a walk on the beach. It was a Thursday afternoon and everyone else was at school or work, so the beach was deserted. The sky was overcast after the previous night's rain and the sand was brown, mushy and sopping wet. Esther screamed past me, boldly jumping off the edges of sand drifts. She crashed so many times that her pink dress looked more like a brown dress with pink spots.

Finally I snagged her, and she squealed and wriggled in my grasp like a wild animal that didn't want to be caught. I awkwardly scraped the wet clothes off the tiny bucking girl, leaving only her diaper on, then set her down. She stood for a moment, fat hands clasped behind her naked potbelly. The humidity stuck her blonde baby curls to the back of her chubby neck. Suddenly and silently, warm rain began pelting the beach.

"Esther, the rain!" I exclaimed. "Do you feel the rain, baby?" I opened my hands to catch the drops, and she mimicked me with her small, plump hands. As soon as a drop kissed her hand, her blue eyes popped in surprise and her eyebrows raised.

She gasped with an open mouth, showing her new white baby teeth. "Wain," she whispered reverently, as if she was in a magical church service. She started running in no particular pattern, her wet baby skin gleaming. The rain slowly smashed her hair down onto her neck and across her forehead in straggly pieces. Then she bolted straight into the ocean waves, scaring me half to death. (She has zero fear of the water.)

I sprinted after her like a nervous Tennessee high-walker horse, pulling my legs up out of the water with each step to move quickly. A big wave tossed her onto her back, rolling her over, then spit her out on her belly. She raised her head, laughing, as salt water streamed down her face. I scooped up her Cabbage Patch Doll body and set her down on her feet on the sand.

It was as if she was a wind-up toy and my holding her had rewound her. *Zoom*, she was off again. "Wah! Wah!" she screamed, squatting with her hands on her little knees. She looked like a tiny dot on a mammoth empty beach.

"I'm watching, baby!" I yelled through the raindrops.

Her trick? She simply jumped up with hands raised, then waited for my response.

I hooted and applauded as if she'd won an Olympic medal. Then she scraped fistfuls of the dark sand and threw them down as hard as she could, over and over. They splattered terrifically on the ground and speckled her skin with flecks of muddy black sand. Soon she looked like a bad Picasso, but I didn't stop her. When else would she get to run free and naked on a deserted beach?

Finally, we were both wet and shivering. I pulled my dirty, naked, wet hooligan up to my chest and felt her heart racing against me and her warm breath on my neck. I kissed her sandy, delicious fat baby cheek, and we started our trek home, a thirty-something mama and a muddy little girl in the gentle rain. These are truly the best days of my life.

Stop and Smell:

I thought I was a confident person until I became a parent. I feel so insecure many days, trying my hardest to do the best job I can, but often feeling guilty and lost. I need encouragement, and today I want to encourage you! I wish I could look you straight in the eye and tell you these words: "You are a good mama." Your days may be long, isolated and full of hard work that no one sees. Listen to me: You are doing a great job. Your children are blessed to have *you* as their mother. God chose *you* for your family and no one else. You are the perfect person for the job. Today when you stopped to listen to that uninteresting toddler story? You were amazing. Last night when you got up at 4 a.m. to care for a little one with love? I was so impressed. Tomorrow when you laugh instead of cry when everything unravels? You'll be the kind of mama that will change tomorrow's world.

Stop and Reflect:

1. What is your favorite part about this season of young children?

2. What do you want to remember about these short, fleeting years? Write down some of your own stories. They may be your favorite book someday.

3. If you are pregnant, what do you look forward to in your new life with a baby?

CHAPTER THIRTY-ONE

The Kind Of Mom I Want To Be

"Motherhood: All love begins and ends there."

–Robert Browning

One thing that helps me with my attitude and my actions is to remind myself about the kind of mom I want to be. The fantasy mom I wish I could be every moment of each day, no matter how tired or stressed I am. Am I this mom? No. I yell at my kids. I get angry at the messes. I get frustrated at the interruptions. I get mad at my husband. But when I pause to think of my ideal mom, it helps. I have a better chance of responding like her when my day unravels, instead of just being a byproduct of circumstances.

The kind of mom I want to be loves her children to the moon back and tells them so—not just once a week, but every day. She kisses her children at odd times, such as giving a slow peck on the forehead in the Target grocery department. She gets on her knees to examine a dead roly poly bug in the parking lot of Chili's on a weekday night. I want to smile all the time and joke around with my children even if the humor is simple. I want to build a positive, happy family culture and make a home, not just a house.

The kind of mom I want to be greets her family when they come home. She makes a big deal about someone's return, greeting them with a hug and happy words, lighting up like greeting a returning soldier. (And if you think about it, our little family fights their own battles in the dark world and we welcome them home after battle.) I started working on this when Samson was a baby. I didn't really feel like stopping what I was doing and lugging the baby downstairs to greet Dave when he got home. But I was determined to develop the heart of our home, making it a welcoming, loving place to return to from the outside world. Some days I am better at it than others, but if I forget, my two little ones help me remember. They go crazy when they hear the garage door open. "Daddy's home! Daddy's home!" When Samson walks in the door with Dad from an errand, I love hearing him yell, "Mama! We hooome! We hooome!" waiting for a response.

The kind of mom I want to be plans her days with life perspective. My mother recognized this dynamic when she raised her five children. My dad worked long hours on weekdays, so his time at home was limited. She toted all five children—we were home-schooled so the older ones went along as well—on errands during the week so that the weekends could be fully devoted to soaking up every minute with Dad and family. She would much rather have been there in the moment on a Saturday morning with her little family than running errands by herself. She knew the season was short and she didn't want to miss it. She was wise beyond her time as a young mother. Today she is a beloved Grandmommy who looks back on her life with satisfaction instead of regret. My mom is the kind of mom I want to be.

The kind of mom I want to be puts relationships above tasks whenever she is able. There will always be tasks. She cares more about reading a picture book with her toddler or playing Transformers with her preschooler than she does about elaborate meals.

The kind of wife I want to be notices her husband, even in the diaper chaos. I want to walk past our little darlings to push him against a wall and kiss him like it was our last kiss. I want to be the kind of wife who can't wait to jump in bed with him at night to share stories about the day. I don't want to get my feelings hurt over petty things like him not asking me a question about my day or not holding my hand in the car. I want to initiate a flirty text message conversation when I'm tired or throw a pillow at him in the mornings just to joke around, even when the floor is covered in toys.

Finally, I want to smile—always smile. It makes me happier and reminds me of the kind of wife and mom I want to be: a happy, bursting flower of sunshine to my family.

Stop and Smell: Have you ever stopped to think about the type of parent you want to be to your children right now? Not the kind of parent you want to be for your child's entire lifespan, but the type of parent you want to be tomorrow with your children at their current ages. Think about it. How can you take steps to becoming that parent?

Stop and Reflect:

1. What qualities are important to you as a mom?

2. Who are some of your role models for being a good mom?

TO BE CONTINUED ...

Dearest reader, after I finished my final read-through of this manuscript, I burst into tears. I suddenly realized what this book was all about: it details my gritty parenting struggles, the hard lessons I learned and ultimately the parenting perspective I gained. I was embarrassed to read some of my struggles. I was sad at how long it took me to learn some lessons. But mostly, I was overwhelmed with gratitude for the kind people who held my hand on my parenting journey.

That's what I hope this book has been for you: a cheerful hand to hold while parenting the little years. These are the best or worst days of our life, depending on our perspective.

Parenting and enjoying small children is still not easy for me. I struggle to enjoy my children in the middle of little-people messes, chaos and stress. (I am also privately worried someone will now observe parenting author Leah yelling at Samson in a Target parking lot for not getting in the car faster. Ha!) So if you have a bad parenting day after reading this book, don't worry, and don't feel guilty! It's normal to mess up. We're human. And this season can be rough.

I sure wish I could meet you and your darling child. I wish I could be a fly on your wall and watch those sweet, private moments you share with your child. I know you are doing a great job!

The little years are a once-in-a-lifetime gift. The days are long, but the years are short. They will be gone before we know it. Let's laugh and enjoy this gift from God.

ABOUT THE AUTHOR

Leah Spina was born in Austin, Texas. Her parents home-educated Leah and her four younger siblings through high school. She started freelance writing as a teenager and also enjoyed competing in golf, tennis and chess tournaments. She graduated from Thomas Edison State College with a Bachelor of Science in Business Administration.

Leah graduated from World Journalism Institute in Asheville, North Carolina, and then worked as a reporter for WORLD magazine, a national news weekly magazine, covering a variety of topics from presidential campaigns to international child support battles. She also worked for the Gladney Center for Adoption in Fort Worth, Texas—one of the nation's largest adoption agencies. She served both as a house parent, caring for expectant and new mothers living at the residential dorm, and as a labor and delivery coach, assisting bedside at over fifty client births. (That's where she discovered the power of the epidural.) Leah still has tremendous respect for the adoption community—especially for teenage mothers who choose to give their babies life, and for the adoptive parents who provide loving homes.

Leah met her husband, David Spina, in 2006 when he delivered a sizzling business presentation while she was sitting in the front row. They dated one year before David proposed to her at a work conference in front of fifteen hundred people, so she had to say yes. They have been married for six years and enjoy playing ice hockey, softball and tennis together. (However, they are both fiercely competitive so sometimes it doesn't end well.)

Since birthing two beautiful blonde children, Leah now spends most of her time primarily feeding and diapering the family she created. She resides in the blistering hot Dallas/Fort Worth, Texas metroplex, where summers are calculated by the number of days over one hundred degrees. (Yes, you will actually see business men in downtown Dallas dressed in suits and boots.)

When Leah's not burning macaroni and cheese, she enjoys riding horses, primarily English riding and jumping, while sporting a soft black velvet helmet and shiny tall boots. (Think housewife turned wanna-be Olympic equestrian champion.) She loves to sing Broadway and travel to Europe, especially to isolated Italian pebble beaches. Leah also enjoys leading Bible studies for mothers of young children at her church, Gateway Church, and downing inordinate amounts of Starbucks caffeine.

To read more parenting stories like these,
visit leahspina.com for Leah's latest parenting
blogs, Leahtube videos and to connect with other
moms of young children.

Come join us!